Bios

DATE DUE

A Year at a Time

Walter Alston

with
JACK TOBIN

A Year
at a Time

WORD BOOKS, Publisher   Waco, Texas

Grateful acknowledgment is
made to the publisher for permission
to use several New York Post photographs by
Stein, © 1954, New York Post Corporation.

ISBN 0-87680-413-X
Library of Congress catalog card number: 75-36194
Printed in the United States of America

To baseball—

Whether it be family, owners, manage-
ment, staff, players, coaches, trainers,
secretaries, spectators, superstars or
substitutes—my thanks for making these
wonderful years possible.

1

ONCE YOU TURN off the Ohio Turnpike north of Cincinnati and bypass Riverfront Stadium, you're getting into my country. It's a route I know better than the playing fields of the National League. Each fall for the past forty years I've taken it home from the baseball season just as the leaves are shading from green to yellow to gold to burnt orange to red to brown . . . almost the whole range of the color spectrum.

It's a fine time of year in Ohio, and there's something about going home to Darrtown that spells peace, security and solitude. I'm still so much of a country boy that when I leave the turnpike and head northwest up U.S. 127 toward Hamilton and Oxford I get downright itchy for the turnoff to Darrtown.

Over the years, especially since I've been manager of the Dodgers—both in Brooklyn and Los Angeles—they've ribbed me a great deal about the size of Darrtown. One of the writers needles me continually. "If you blink your eyes, Walter," he tells me, "you'll miss all of Darrtown." He's not too far from right.

Darrtown sits about eight miles north of Hamilton and five miles east of Oxford. It's Middle America. Maybe, if we count the cars and the dogs and the horses, there are about three hundred of us. To me it's God's country. But I admit to being biased. I was born and raised and will probably die amid that rolling farm land. I've walked or ridden a horse or driven a car over almost every square inch of Butler County.

When you come right down to it, the biggest single moment of my life took place in Darrtown. Now some will wonder about that, pointing to National League pennants, World Series Championships and Manager of the Year awards and other

7

wonderful things that have happened to me in my lifetime. But none of it would have been possible if I hadn't been in Darrtown and known the Reverend Ralph Jones.

I'd graduated from Milford Township High School in Darrtown on May 18, 1929. That fall I enrolled at Miami University in Oxford, Ohio. A month later the bottom fell out of the stock market and the Great Depression was upon us. By the end of my freshman year I knew there was no way I could afford to go back to college.

Lela and I were married that May—May 10, 1930, to be exact. We lived with Lela's parents, the Alexanders, and I worked where I could: day-to-day farm chores in the area; when it was needed, cutting roadside weeds for the county with a big hand scythe. That paid a dollar a day and I was happy to have it.

One hot day in the summer of 1932—the rock-bottom pit of the depression—I was swinging that big, long-handled sickle when Rev. Jones stopped to chat. He was the minister of the Methodist Church where I went to Sunday school and my folks attended services.

I remember very well how at Sunday school Rev. Jones stressed time and again the value of education and how he was always on us to be sure and get our high school diploma.

As I stood there in the broiling sun, leaning on the scythe and happy to have a break, we talked about what I was doing and what I wanted to do. He'd found out that I had dropped out of college but I was kind of surprised when he asked me to come by and see him.

A few days later I dropped by and we talked. As usual, he pointed out the value of a college education, how I had a year in, and what a shame it would be not to complete work for my degree. He knew the problems of going to college in those days. There were no athletic scholarships; part-time jobs were full time for whoever could find them, no matter what they paid; and it certainly wasn't possible for my dad or Lela's dad to give us any more help.

Rev. Jones talked for quite a while. He pointed out that Lela and I could continue to live with our parents (hers or mine), commute back and forth to Oxford and somehow scrape by while I got my degree in education. "I can't help you very much," said this kindly man, "but here is fifty dollars. That will help pay your tuition."

Classes weren't too far away. I went home and talked it over with Lela and my dad. Lela felt it was the thing to do. Dad knew it was because he knew of my great desire to play baseball. I decided to try and make it one way or the other. So, with Rev. Jones's fifty dollars, I went over to Miami and enrolled for the fall semester of 1932.

Today, if it hadn't been for Rev. Jones's timely gift, I'd probably be a farmer somewhere near Darrtown. We never could have saved fifty dollars on my dollar a day cutting weeds. Not in a time when you guarded nickels like you do a hundred-dollar bill today.

If that still doesn't make sense to you, remember Darrtown was much smaller then than now, and there weren't any scouts at the Milford Township High School baseball games. Had Rev. Jones not provided me with that boost to return to college I would not have had a chance to play baseball. Even at Miami University there weren't many scouts in those days, but there were a lot more than around Darrtown. By returning to school I was able not only to play baseball but basketball, and to get a degree and achieve the goal that Rev. Jones constantly talked about.

I've only one regret about Rev. Jones's kindness. I never really found out why he gave me the fifty dollars. That little Methodist Church didn't take in much on the Sunday collection, and ministers sure didn't make much then, so it had to be a great personal sacrifice. I would like to know why Rev. Jones picked out Walter Alston.

That's impossible now. Rev. Jones is gone, and I can only speculate as to why he decided to take me under his wing. It was tough in those days for young people even to get through high school. Rev. Jones was a man of strong principle, strong ambition, and strong feeling about education. Maybe he was impressed that I was the only one from my time who'd gone on to college. And I'd gotten off to a pretty good start, both academically and in basketball and baseball.

I've got to conclude that he believed he was making a worthwhile investment. I know it was, and I make sure each year that little white-steepled church gets considerably more than the sum that wonderful man gave me.

Don't let me mislead anyone. That fifty dollars didn't get me *through* college; it got me back in and paid a good part of my tuition for that year. (I don't rightly recall the exact tuition cost then at Miami, but it probably came to thirty-five or forty dollars a year.)

Living at home in Darrtown, I had an old Model T Ford that got me back and forth. I had two other jobs during the school year, and once I was back at the university I was able to get a student loan each year. The loan total got up to $400 at graduation—a fortune in those days—but that college degree and the other opportunities it brought were worth every bit of sacrifice we made.

Looking back, as I do every time I make that Darrtown turn, I realize again and again how many wonderful things in my life have happened because of Rev. Ralph Jones and his fifty dollars.

2

I WASN'T BORN IN Darrtown, but on a small farm near Venice, Ohio, a town about twenty miles south of there. Venice isn't on the map any more; they changed its name to Ross several years ago.

My parents, William Emmons Alston and Lenora Neanover Alston, lived in a small tenant farmer's house on the place where Dad worked for the owner. I was born on December 1, 1911, and they named me Walter Emmons.

All I know of Venice and the farm that was my birthplace is what my mom and dad told me. I've been by it many times but it's not a real part of my memory book.

The first place I actually remember was at Jericho, where we lived next. You wouldn't need any walls around this one: there were only three houses there at the time. Ours had two stories, and I thought it was huge. It's been added onto a time or two since and looks pretty nice. My grandparents—Mom's folks, the Neanovers—lived just over a little knoll and it was a big treat for Mom or Dad to take me over there. I still remember those visits, but my most vivid memory from those very early years was of Dad getting kicked by one of his horses. He was husking corn about a half mile from the house. He had the team harnessed up to a wagon and as he moved through the field husking, first he'd tell the team to move on, and then he'd give 'em "whoa" to stop. He didn't have to drive them or anything; they just knew what their job was.

This day one of them must have been kind of lazy. When Dad told them to "git," one didn't and he popped him on the rump with his hand. The horse gave Dad a good kick that broke his jaw and knocked him out, as well as all his teeth on one side. It was a long time before he came to and finally dragged himself to the house. When Mom saw how badly he was bleeding she drove him over to Granddad's place and they took him to the nearest doctor—in Somerville, three or four miles east of the farm.

I was only three or four when we left that farm, and that's pretty young, but I'll remember one day there forever. It was cold and Dad had his heavy sheepskin coat on when he came home. He told me to put my hand in his pocket. I reached in and pulled out a tiny little bundle of fur. It was a young collie pup, just about weaned. There wasn't a happier kid in the world than me right then.

We called the puppy Shep, and he was with us for almost nineteen years, moving from farm to farm and finally to Darrtown. Shep was a great farm dog. Dad trained him to bring in the cows and the horses. If Dad wanted the horses he just whistled and off Shep would go to round them up. I'm not sure how he knew whether he was being asked to get the cows or the horses unless it was the time of day. Along about time to milk, Shep would take off and nip at the cows until they'd fall in line and he could herd them into the barn. He did that every day as long as we were on the farm.

11

My interest in hunting was born on this farm. Dad came home one day with a BB gun and taught me how to shoot. He'd put tin cans up on a post and teach me how to lead. I got pretty good at knocking the tin cans off but not before Dad got tired of putting them up. Then he hung a can from a wire and I'd sit out there hours at a time pinging away at it. Fortunately, BBs came cheap then. At the store you'd get enough for a nickel to last a long time.

When I got so I could hit the tin can while it was swinging I picked up enough of an edge to go after a mean old rooster that loved to chase me. Up until then it seemed like he'd kind of lie in wait to sneak up on me. Then when I'd get close, he'd peck at my heels and send me running into the house. Now I'd let him chase me, usually when I was going to the outhouse. I'd really have to haul the mail to get there ahead of him. Then I'd bang the door closed, wait a bit, then crack it just enough to stick the barrel out and dare that old rooster to come near me. I'd plink away at him, but he'd stay his distance so it'd hardly ruffle his feathers when I hit him.

When I was between five and six we moved to a farm about four miles north of Jericho and nine to ten miles south of Camden.

By then I was big enough to do some chores, and one of the daily ones was to walk out and see if we'd gotten any mail. I had to feed the horses every morning and night. Each one of them got a couple of ears of corn, some hay and some oats. As I got older I'd climb up in the silo and throw the silage out for the cows. Dad usually spread it around. The only cows I milked were the more gentle ones, and never more than two or three a day. Usually, while Mom and Dad finished up the milking, I cranked the cream separator. After that was done we'd feed the milk to our hogs and keep the cream to make butter with, use on our cereal or to whip for topping on pies. If we had surplus cream Dad would take it in to town and trade it for groceries.

The garden was Mom's task, with a little help from me. Dad would always use the team to plow the ground up but Mom did the planting. We raised all our own vegetables—potatoes, onions, lettuce, beets, carrots, peas, green beans, sweet corn, the usual garden plot. The hoeing was all mine and I'm afraid that

I chopped down about as many plants as I did weeds. The watering we left to God.

Back in those days we had to worry about the winter. There was no refrigeration so everybody had cellars for keeping potatoes, parsnips and other things—like apples—as long as you could. Mom canned everything you could think of, fruits as well as vegetables.

Apples were always plentiful and good. We'd swap around for peaches, apricots and plums when we could. We'd grow a few berries but a lot of the time we'd just go out in the woods and pick wild berries. Man, they made wonderful pies.

Our meals weren't too fancy but they sure were good. We had our own meat, and Mother made great homemade bread. It smelled so good it always brought me running in for a hot slice with sugar and butter on it. I think one of the great disappointments in my dad's life was when Mother quit baking it.

We'd been on the second farm a year or so when Dad got me a coal black Shetland pony. I called her Night. The first place I rode Night was around the barn area near the house. Then I stretched things out a bit by riding her out to the mail box every day to see if anything had come. I'd guess the mail box was perhaps a half mile—maybe a quarter mile—out on the dirt road.

When I got a little older, maybe eight or so, I'd climb up on Night and ride all the way in to Somerville to the grocery for Mom. That was really great. A nice ride. I'd guess it would take me an hour or two. I had a sack that I could put around Night's neck to bring the groceries back in.

Dad was doing pretty well on that farm, not making a great deal of hard cash, but the crops were good and we lived well. Then after about four years someone convinced him to move onto a larger farm just across the road and down a piece near Morning Sun.

It was more than double the size of the one we'd been on— around 280 acres, I'd guess—and it involved a lot of extra expense. Dad had to buy another team of horses; in fact, three more horses. He also had to buy a wheat binder and hire a man to help him, going into debt to do all this.

It was a big farm with big buildings. The barn was a beauty —big even by today's standards—and the land was excellent.

13

It was rolling country and had a nice woods on it where I used to go hunting for fire wood, and hunting, period.

Those days I was up long before daylight. Dad would set some traps for me in the woods—for skunks and possums or whatever—and I'd ride down in the woods and run my traps before daylight. Then I'd come back to the barn, milk my cows, grab breakfast, and take off for school.

Shortly after we moved to the big farm, Dad had arranged a transfer for me to go to school in Morning Sun since it was only three miles from our house. He also built a little old buggy for me which Night could pull at a pretty good clip. So now instead of having to be out on the road in the dark in order to cover those nine miles in the horse bus to Camden, Night could get me to Morning Sun in a few minutes if I wanted to run her pretty good.

Every Monday I'd load the buggy with enough corn to feed Night for the week. Then I'd drive into Morning Sun to the barn where they kept the bus wagon. During the week the driver would feed Night, and all I'd have to do then was to walk about a quarter of a mile to school. The rest of the week I'd ride Night back and forth unless Mom wanted a load of groceries. Then I'd take the buggy so I could carry them.

The buggy was a beauty and so was Night. Dad was real handy with his hands, and he had painted the buggy black and trimmed it in red. It just matched Night's coat and it looked just elegant.

It wasn't too long after we moved onto that 280 acres and Dad went up to his ears in hock for equipment that the post-World War I recession hit. I'd guess it was about 1922 or 1923. He went deeper and deeper in debt. All the farmers were in the same boat. Prices fell way down and you couldn't sell your crops or even try swapping corn or hogs for the staples you needed to live on.

I remember the day Dad decided to sell. The latest paper he'd seen listed hogs at eighteen cents a pound. The day he sold they started at seven cents and by the time he sold they were down to three.

That did it. They held an auction on the farm and he sold everything—horses, cows, pigs, all his equipment. The only things he saved were our clothes, the household furnishings,

Night, and my dog, Shep. I don't think he had ten cents in cash when we left that big farm and moved into Darrtown for the first time.

Dad was fortunate enough to find a job shortly after that with the Ford Motor Company in Hamilton, eight miles away. It paid him four dollars a day and he was mighty happy to get it. Still, with ten dollars a month rent to pay for the little bungalow he'd found us, there wasn't much left to erase that $2400 debt. It was a great day several years later when he could finally tell us that he'd paid it off and was going to start saving to buy a lot and build a house.

3

BASEBALL has been part of me as far back as I can remember. Dad loved the game. Even though farmers in those days worked from dawn to dark and beyond, they played a lot of ball on Sundays. Dad was on various town teams in the area over the years.

My first personal recollection of baseball comes from the time when we moved to our second farm, the one south of Camden, where we lived when I started to school. One of the buildings on the farm was a smokehouse, built just like a blockhouse, with thick brick walls. It was probably just a little less than twenty feet high and about ten or twelve feet wide, with fairly level ground in front of it. That's where I started playing baseball.

Somewhere Dad had found a little glove for me and I'd stand out there by the hour throwing a hard rubber ball against the smokehouse wall, fielding the grounders or catching the ball on the fly if it didn't go too far over my head.

Like every kid, I'd get tired of that and would go around picking up rocks and hitting them out with a broomstick. I'd even hit corn grains from out around the corn crib and the silo. When you'd connect with them you'd feel pretty good about it because they were so darn small.

Dad would play catch with me whenever he had time but that wasn't too often, because it seemed he was always a day and a half behind. I remember there was a door into the barn—one that a man could walk in—that Dad said was just about the size of the strike zone. He'd get out there and throw to me. If the ball hit the lower part of the door it was a strike. He could put a lot on the ball in those days, and if I'd hit a few he'd put a little extra juice on it and the ball would just bang into the door.

We wore out many a barn door because every time the ball slammed into it the wood would splinter a little bit more. It wouldn't be long until we'd knock the cover off the ball. We'd tape it up a bit or tie it up and go right ahead. Finally it would get so soft that you couldn't hit it a lick. But I never remember being out of baseballs. Dad used to get the culls from whatever team he played for.

When Dad got weary of pitching—and I'd stay up against the barn door all day hitting—we'd go out to a fairly level field near the house and he'd hit fungoes out to me. I was pretty good at catching the ball, but when you're five or six or so your arm isn't too strong, so Mother would be the halfway man to relay the ball back in to Dad.

You know, looking back on it, I have to admit she had a pretty good arm. I know she could throw as long as I could until I got up around ten or twelve.

When we moved to Darrtown, Dad played a lot more baseball. Having a job at Ford with regular hours left him more free time to play. The first year we lived in Darrtown—I was in the seventh grade so I was about twelve—someone hit a foul ball in a town game. I hadn't had a new baseball in a long time. I chased that ball down and took off toward home. Dad never said anything about it, but odds are he paid for the ball.

Back in those days town teams in baseball were big. Every town, no matter what size it was, had a town team. You know they were important, because when they played it was usually on Sunday and everyone from both towns would turn out.

16

About this time the Armco Steel team from down in Middletown came to Darrtown to play. Charlie Root, who was then pitching for the Chicago Cubs, was born and raised in Middletown. During the off season he pitched for Armco Steel. When they played Darrtown, Root won it for Armco.

Darrtown got a return match and the folks in town were so involved with the game that they collected a hundred dollars and hired Hod Eller, who used to pitch for Cincinnati. It was some game. Eller, who was a big right-hander about the same size and just as fast as Root, beat Root's team, 2–1.

My dad, Uncle Stanley Alston, and Uncle Paul Neanover played for Darrtown. Even though most of the team was made up of fellows you had never heard of, they were a little better than average. They loved the game and really worked at it.

There were teams everywhere. Seven Mile had a team. So did Somerville, Scipio, Collinsville, Oxford, Middletown—all the towns around. The fans would flock from all over and line up along the foul lines. I've got photographs of the Eller-Root game with horse-drawn buggies, Model Ts, and hundreds of people lined all the way around the field.

I dreamed as a kid of being a ball player. I can remember going by Miami University during baseball season and seeing the college teams playing. I can remember thinking, "Gee, those guys are good," and wondering if some day *I* might be that good.

I know I have always loved baseball. Not only as a game to watch but especially a game to play. There was no TV when I was growing up and we didn't have a radio until after we had been in Darrtown a few years. It was quite a while before I could listen to the Cincinnati or Cleveland games. Once we got one, though, it was on every day I was home. Night ball, of course, hadn't had its first major league game yet.

One of the greatest days of my life came when I was about ten years old and we were still on the farm. Dad took me to Cincinnati to see major league baseball, an exhibition between the Reds and the New York Yankees, and Babe Ruth was playing.

We got up before it was light. We had to drive in the buggy over to Somerville to borrow Granddad's Model T. Dad wanted to get there in time to see batting practice, but especially infield. In those days the pepper games during batting practice were quite a thing. They'd bounce the ball back and forth with all kinds of fancy didoes and tricky tosses.

It took us several hours to get to Cincinnati and old Crosley Field. We parked in a kind of dug-out place along the railroad tracks near the park.

All I can remember is that the Yankees won the exhibition. Babe Ruth hit a home run and so did the Yankee first baseman. I don't think it was Lou Gehrig, but more likely Wally Pipp, whom Gehrig replaced. I'm just not sure.

It was a long drive home. The roads were dirt, a Model T couldn't go too fast, and because of the lights the driving was even slower when it got dark. I don't remember a thing about the trip back except for how really dark it was when we got back to our farm. I was asleep most of the way.

That was the only major league game I ever saw until after I had signed.

I lived on the memories of Ruth, the Yankees and the Reds for months, playing imaginary baseball games in which I was usually the pitcher, and I always won.

AS IN MOST small Ohio towns, school in those days took in everything from the first grade through high school. I don't remember how many kids were in my class then, but it wasn't many. At recess we played baseball during the season for it and after that we played basketball.

We used a little ball diamond that was on the school grounds. The town team had one in a field on the outskirts of town, though for a couple of years they used a diamond that my great-uncle, Andy Neanover, had out on his farm. That's where Root and Eller fought their little duel.

It was really a field on which they had mowed the grass, skinned off the base paths and put up a makeshift backstop to catch some of the passed balls and foul tips.

Baseball was big in those days with kids, a lucky thing since it would take all the boys in school to make up a ball team. I was always pretty good size for my age, and long before I got into high school I was playing baseball with the bigger kids. At that time there were probably two hundred people, kids and all, in Darrtown, so there was no surplus of players. Fact is, there were times when we had to shift the outfield depending on whether there was a right-handed or a left-handed batter up. We'd usually be short a man or two and sometimes more than that. Most of the kids in school came from neighboring farms and sometimes they had to take an early bus in order to get home.

Basketball was the big thing in the winter, but when I was in the seventh and eighth grades Darrtown didn't have any indoor facility for it. By the time I reached high school they had remodeled the auditorium into two convertible classrooms that could be made into a gym or an auditorium.

Before we had that we played basketball outside on a cinder court. There were many times it was pretty cold, but we'd play anyway, doing our best to keep our hands warm. We usually just stuck our hands in our pockets.

We were all sure proud of the new indoor basketball court with the divided classroom. I can remember every morning we'd move all the desks and the chairs out in the hall so we could play basketball before classes. Then we'd have to move them back in. They put up wire mesh screens on the inside of the windows so we wouldn't break the glass.

When basketball season was on we'd have to do the same thing after school for the team to practice and straighten it up again before we could go home. And it had to get done before the bus left with the kids who didn't live right in Darrtown but out on farms.

As an auditorium it had a small stage at one end and could seat an audience of about twenty-five. For basketball, backboards and baskets, not quite full size, were built and hung up. People could only stand one deep around the edges so if we could get a hundred in for a game we were lucky. It wasn't a regulation court by far. The playing floor wasn't very long. It

19

had only about fifteen feet between the foul circles. The first year an electric generator in the basement provided power. The lights weren't good and the first time I played on a real court I was surprised how well you could see the basket. The next year we had electricity put in.

The ceiling was pretty low. Then, since the room wasn't built as a gym, the backboards had to be cut down from the standard size in order for the hoop to be ten feet off the floor. As I recall, after they'd made the boards to regulation size, they had to saw an inch or two off the top to get the hoop into the proper relationship of height off the floor and distance to the top of the board. Your shots had to have a pretty flat trajectory or they'd hit the ceiling. When you got to play on a regulation court somewhere it was a problem.

I remember I had a little trouble with Dad over basketball. Basketball in Ohio is as big as in Indiana—which is right next door—but the first time Dad went to a game and saw all the guys running around in short pants he didn't go for it too much. Finally he agreed to let me play, and once I started he never missed a game either in Darrtown or in the towns nearby. About the only games he missed were those when he was on the night shift at Ford.

There were only four classrooms, a basement where they had woodshop and home ec, and the office. As I remember, one classroom handled all the grades from one through six. Then one handled the seventh and eighth, with the rest being the high school.

Our eighth-grade teacher must have been glad to see me go on to high school. One day she made me stay in at noon as punishment for something. As she stood in front of the door watching the class file out, I slipped into the cloakroom, which had an emergency outside door, and out I went.

The next day she made me stay in for the day I skipped out. This time she kept her eye on the cloakroom but I went out the fire escape.

The third day she thought she had every avenue covered. But it was warm and the windows were up, so I just hoisted myself through the window and dropped the two or three feet to the ground. That day she came up into town to get me.

There wasn't any more to downtown Darrtown then than

there is now: just a general store where you could get ice cream and Coke, the Knights of Pythias Hall, and a gas pump. In fact, it wasn't more than a block from school but that's where the teacher corraled me.

High school in Darrtown—correctly, Milford Township High School—was pretty basic. We had none of the frills of today. Heck, how could we; it was a very small school district, with very few children and not too many tax dollars coming in. I didn't realize it then but the teachers were probably working for $1,000 a year or maybe even less.

We had no labs for chemistry or any of the other sciences, but by the time I was a senior they'd put a little woodworking equipment down in the basement—just a few of the normal hand tools like saws, chisels, planes, brace and bit. My interest in woodworking stems from that time.

The only foreign language they taught was Latin. I took it or it took me, I don't know which. For most of the time in school I did what I had to do and not much more, but along about my junior year at Milford Township I got a little more serious about classwork. I'd see the Miami students playing basketball and baseball. And I knew I wanted to give that a crack so I had to get some grades in order to get into college. By the time I was a senior I was doing much better. One time I was even on the six-week honor roll.

After we moved into Darrtown I looked forward to the summers. I missed the farm and all it meant, even though most of it was work, especially in those months. When I was in high school Granddad was still on a farm, and I'd go out there to spend maybe a month or more working for him during the busy part of the season.

I'd help him cultivate the corn, spending many a day behind a walking plow or, in my younger years when I couldn't walk all day long, riding a single-row plow. You'd sit on this single seat behind the horse and guide the plow with your feet to keep from cutting through the corn row or covering up the young sprouts. My last year or two of high school, I'd pitch hay with a fork at haying time. That was rugged work, but Granddad paid me a dollar a day plus room and board.

But there was also baseball during the summer vacations in high school, and I played a lot with various teams. The Baldwin

Grocery team, which was sponsored by a store in Hamilton, was one I remember especially because my dad, my uncles, and I all played on the same club. My Alston uncle—Stanley, who almost everybody called Doc—as well as Uncle Paul Neanover and Dad were on this team. I was the shortstop this particular year and we won the championship.

Our high school did pretty well winning titles too. In basketball, even in our little old crackerbox of a convertible gym, the four years that we played there we were undefeated in our gym. Since at 6-2 I was the biggest guy in school, I played center on the team. My senior year, as I recall, we beat Jackson High, 74–10. I scored 60 points myself, my all-time high. We won twelve straight games to go into the district championships at Hamilton.

In the finals for the county championship we met West Chester, the defending champions. We were ahead by nine points in that game, which was a pretty safe lead in those days. I already had three fouls of the four we were allowed.

West Chester was going down on a fast break and I had my back to the ball. One of their guards hit me with it while trying to make a long pass. When the referee called me for face guarding it put me out of the game on four fouls and probably cost us the tournament championship.

I've never let him forget it. It was Frank Lane, one of baseball's more famous general managers, especially during his days at Cleveland.

Every time I run into him, usually at the winter baseball meetings, I josh him about it. If we'd won that game—and I think we would have if I hadn't been thrown out on fouls—we'd have gone to the state tournament.

That was pretty good for so small a school as Milford Township. There were only eight of us in our graduating class—five girls and three boys—and not much more than twenty boys all told in the whole school.

The year that West Chester beat us, I made the All-County team at center and Cliff Alexander, later my brother-in-law, made the second team at forward. Clarence Wright, who became a career Navy man after high school, made honorable mention at guard.

Cliff, who was two years behind me in school, was a fine

22

basketball and baseball player. He pitched for Darrtown while I was there and then went on to Miami U. after I graduated. He was good enough to sign and played a couple years of minor league ball. He had a real fine arm and could really zing the ball until he hurt it. Cliff passed away during the 1975 baseball season with cancer. He was a scout for the Dodgers for years, though at the time of his death he worked for Cincinnati.

When I was at Portsmouth, either in 1938 or 1939, he was pitching against us for Canton. The first time he faced me he stuck a good fast ball in my ribs. Later in the same game I doubled off him down the left field line and went to third on an infield out. There were two outs, the game was tied and just as he wound up to pitch I hollered, "Hey, Cliff, wait a minute!"

He hesitated just enough to commit a balk. I walked home with the winning run. I figured I'd gotten even with him pretty good for sticking me in the ribs. Now, however, the rules prohibit the base runner from distracting the pitcher in any manner.

Our baseball team did a little better than basketball. My senior year we won the county championship, beating Oxford. Funny thing is, that was the only season we didn't have our regular coach—a woman history teacher. She made up the batting order and kept score. She was something, even though she couldn't teach us much about baseball except discipline.

There were only eleven of us on the club that year. There were times if a few fellows were sick or had to go home and do some chores we couldn't get nine on the field for practice. I pitched most of the games the year of that championship, and my distant cousin, Stanton Neanover, was the catcher. In fact, he won the championship game for us when he pounded out a triple with the bases full and ended a two-year reign by Monroe. W. H. Ogden, our principal, was the coach replacing our feminine history teacher.

We did pretty well considering the equipment we had. Two or three bats was all. If one broke during the season we'd have to patch it up with some finish nails and tape, if we could. We'd get to use one new ball per game and sometimes they'd be awful dark from dirt and grass stains.

Dad took a great interest in our baseball team. If he was on the night shift he went to every game. He often pitched batting practice to us and was really good. He could move the ball around real well with a little on it so you just weren't hitting lollipops.

One time I ripped one straight back through the mound and it hit him right in the belly. He didn't blink an eye or rub his belly; just picked up the ball and threw me another pitch.

The next day he pulled his shirt up and showed me the result. He was all black and blue. That had been a real shot that hit him but he wasn't going to let on to us kids that his young son could hurt him.

5

THINGS WERE pretty good in the summer of '29, and Dad and Mother agreed that college would be a good thing for me. Miami University was close, and I'd spent a lot of time over there watching the teams play.

In those days the coaches didn't recruit and there were no scholarship offers. If you were good enough and your parents could afford it they'd like to have you. So I spent the summer working on Granddad Charlie Neanover's farm and wherever else I could find a day's work or two. When the fall semester opened, I was ready with my tuition money.

Football was the big thing on campus at the beginning of the school year, but before long the call for basketball practice went out and I reported. I thought I was pretty good. Darrtown had done real well in the county tournament. I had enough size that I figured I could play forward or guard for Miami.

Just about that time came Black Friday and the 1929 market crash. I really didn't know what it meant. But soon students were dropping out of school. Their fathers had lost jobs, and money was short. Gradually the impact began to sink in. Dad didn't express any great concern. He was still working for Ford so I went on about college life and especially basketball.

I soon found out there was more to the game than I'd thought. At Darrtown you went out and played basketball. If you played it better than anyone else you were first team. No one ever told me to do something this way or that way. I'd never had a lesson on how to dribble a basketball, how to shoot or rebound or anything. I just played.

After a couple of weeks at Miami I'd learned more about the game than in all four years in high school. I was really a greenhorn when it came to the intricate techniques of the game.

About a month after practice started, we scrimmaged the varsity. I grabbed off a varsity pass and when one of their guards forced me wide a bit I put up one of my one-handed shots that went over big in high school and made it.

But the whistle blew. That stopped play. And out I came. Ditmer, the freshman coach, took me aside and explained that such a play might have been OK in high school but not at Miami. He told me that when I was forced out I should have slowed up, waited for my teammates to come down court, and set up to run a play.

That was my first shock. I had thought it was a really great play, intercepting the ball, slipping wide past the guard and scoring two points. But they didn't. It was the wrong way.

In those days freshmen weren't eligible for the varsity although we scrimmaged against them most of the time. We also played a freshman schedule as a preliminary to the varsity and made a trip or two to nearby colleges in Ohio, Indiana and Kentucky.

It was the same in baseball. Freshmen weren't eligible for the varsity but we worked out together. I discovered very early that Frank Wilton knew quite a bit about baseball, although I was sure then, as I am now, that football was his first love.

Nevertheless, Wilton taught me a lot about the game, and I probably knew more about baseball when I went to Miami than I did basketball. I'd learned a great deal about the inside aspects of baseball from my dad. By playing on town teams with him I'd gotten to associate with some pretty good players. All the talking in the world can't teach you as much about technique as visual observation.

25

As a freshman, I did pretty well, playing the infield or pitching. I still had a little of that "smoke" dad used to call for and I'd learned a breaking pitch or two from all those weekend and summer games while playing for clubs like the Baldwin Grocers.

There's no doubt that Dad is the one responsible for my being called Smokey. He seldom called me Walt. It was always, "Smokey, do this," or "Hey, Smokey, get me a pitchfork," so pretty soon everyone around Darrtown was calling me Smokey. I'm not real sure, but I guess it all began when I was just getting big enough to throw with some velocity on the ball. Dad would hold his glove out as a target and say, "Smoke it in here." To this day I hear Smokey from more people in Darrtown than I do Walt.

By the time my freshman year came to an end the full impact of the depression had hit. It was terrible. Stores were closed. Farmers were going broke everywhere. People were being laid off at Ford by the dozens almost every day. Dad was still working but they were beginning to cut his time back, and it was obvious to me that things were going to get worse.

Lela and I had been going together for several years and we had planned to be married when she graduated that year. In spite of the depression we were stubborn as all young people in love can be. We went right ahead with the ceremony, although we didn't tell our parents until after commencement.

Looking back, I guess it wasn't too much of a shock to them. Most people married young in those days, and with the economy what it was, maybe it was best the way we did it. There were several showers for Lela and a reception at her parents' home. We even went over to the Knights of Pythias Hall afterwards for a little dancing, which everyone from Darrtown enjoyed. The whole town was there.

6

THE NEXT TWO years were the toughest of our life, but the severity of the depression didn't hit Lela and me at first. The full impact came only when I went looking for work.

I'd get a day here and a day there but there was no sign of anything steady. I think I did every kind of job there was in and around Darrtown. I was not quite as handy with my hands as Dad but good enough so I could help out at most anything.

And that's what it was—most anything—for a couple of years. Still, living with Lela's folks, we weren't having to pay any rent, and we were getting by. But it was a struggle, and making a buck a day wouldn't let you do too much or go very far.

When Rev. Jones offered me that fifty dollars, I knew it was just about my only chance of going anywhere in the world, so the decision was made for me to return to Miami. Fortunately, we still had the same Model T roadster that had been my transportation to and from Miami my freshman year. It was second or third hand then and, as best I can recall, had cost $75. But it would get me there and back.

The coaches—Maurer and Wilton—both wanted me to come back. Of course, since there was no scholarship help for athletes, they'd try to help us get jobs. I'm sure that's how I got the laundry route I drove every morning around the dorms. Somehow what I made there and by working at Cunningham's luncheonette and pool parlor for ten cents an hour, plus whatever summer work came my way, carried us through.

There is no doubt the two-year layoff helped strengthen my determination to study. I knew it was my last chance for a college education, and the depression made it very obvious how important that education was.

27

It was a good thing I had a farm background. I had to get up before dark in order to make my laundry run and still get to an eight o'clock class. It seemed I had eight o'clocks every year I was at Miami. That meant I had to be up by 5:30 and on my way by 6:00 so I could be starting dorm rounds by 6:30.

In the winter that was tough. There weren't many garages in those days so cars stood out overnight. The temperature would probably be zero or less. I'd be out there cranking and cranking to get the old T started even though I covered it up at night. Many times before I could get it started I had to jack up the hind wheels to make cranking easier. Then I had to let the jack down, leap in and hope the car would take off.

It wasn't as easy or quick to get to Miami as it is now. Then the roads weren't as good and the snow plows not as powerful, so if it was icy you would do a lot of slipping and sliding. I always carried some big cinders in the car in case of slipping on some really slick ice.

Difficult as it all was, I've never been sorry for the decision to go back to school.

One of the bonuses of having a double major in physical education and industrial arts was that I learned a lot about woodworking. Miami has a fine industrial arts program. The woodshop had large table saws, band saws, lathes, large planers and shapers, along with fine hand tools. You could make anything you wanted or were required to make. I really enjoyed it. And much to my surprise I really liked mechanical drawing and became quite proficient in it before I graduated. That part of my education undoubtedly contributed to my having such a large shop today.

The town of Oxford is a perfect little city for a small college. Actually, I guess you can't say Miami is small any more. When I went there it had a student body of probably three thousand or so. Now it's up around thirteen thousand. The campus has a lot of new buildings and the school is talking about building a new football stadium to go along with the new fieldhouse— Millett Hall, where we go to basketball games in the winter. The Miami football field holds only around fifteen thousand spectators.

A lot of famous football names have come from the school

over the years. Earl (Red) Blaik, one of the great football coaches at Army; Paul Brown, whose Cleveland Browns dominated the NFL for years and who is doing real well now with the Cincinnati Bengals; Weeb Ewbank, who was head coach of the New York Jets for years; Sid Gillman, who was with the Rams and the Chargers and Houston; Woody Hayes, who is one of the super coaches at Ohio State.

Then there is Ara Parseghian, who did so well at Notre Dame until he retired. Paul Dietzel, who was at Army for a time. Stu Holcomb, who coached Purdue for years and was later Northwestern athletic director. Johnny Pont, who moved from Indiana to Northwestern. Bo Schembechler, who coached Miami and is now at Michigan. Jack Faulkner, now chief scout with the Rams but who was once head coach with the Denver Broncos. And Miami's long line of good coaches like Blaik, Brown and Hayes have to be up there with the greatest of all time.

It's quite a tradition—one that those of us who went to Miami are proud of. (I guess I've got to be one of the black sheep because I went into baseball. I can't name off a long list of big names like that in baseball but you have to remember that back in my day college baseball wasn't what it is today.)

Miami was no snap for me. I took it seriously, but I remember how tough freshman English was for me. I actually flunked it the first semester of my freshman year and had to do extra work to get through. I finally made it but it's still a big problem for me. I did make good enough grades in the rest of my classes to stay in school and maintain the C+ average required to compete in sports.

Some of the P.E. science courses were tough—kinesiology for one—but I was up near A's in most of them. I remember one of the first lab projects in kinesiology. We didn't have to work on cadavers then but each student had a cat preserved in formaldehyde that we had to skin and dissect. I was way ahead of the class. I'd helped Dad skin coon and possum by the dozen along with rabbits and skunks. Some of those city slicker kids were a little edgy cutting up their cats. I had mine skinned and torn apart before most of them had the hair off.

That's one place where being a farm boy paid off. I had a

tough time pronouncing half the words, but I studied like mad and got A's. I also did well in industrial arts and my other minor, biological science.

Time was my big problem. There wasn't much for leisure. Practice for basketball or baseball usually took a couple of hours at the end of the school day. By the time I'd cranked up the Ford again and driven back to Darrtown it was long past dark. Usually I'd get in around eight for dinner. If I could study for a couple of hours I'd be lucky, because that alarm went off awfully soon.

Basketball always seemed to last longer, mostly, I suppose, because of winter and early sundown. I don't think we worked out any longer than in baseball but in the spring the days were starting to get longer. But the real truth was that, although I really enjoyed basketball, baseball was still my first love.

7

WHEN I REPORTED to John Mauer for basketball practice in the fall of 1932, after being out of school two years, I found out I wasn't in as good shape as I thought. But Mauer, a stern, serious basketball man who really knew the game, was an excellent teacher and helped me immensely to readjust.

During the gradual process of working my way into shape I began to truly appreciate Mauer as a teacher. There had never been any doubt in my mind that he knew the game. But it was his ability to get the message to all of us that really impressed me, and I learned a lot from Mauer about working with players. He had a good psychological approach to players. He knew how to handle them. He knew when to pat them on the back or give them a good swift kick. If you made a bonehead pass or took a wild shot with no one near the boards to rebound he would get a little rough with you. But if you were going full bore on a fast break and just messed up a snap pass he would never criticize you.

We had 21 men out for the varsity and while the roster listed me at 6-2 and 188, that wasn't really fact. I was just a shade over 6-1½ but I was just about even for the biggest man on the squad. To illustrate what a difference two or three generations make, one of Johnny Wooden's All-Americans at UCLA, Gail Goodrich, who they call Stumpy, at 6-1 is one of the great guards of the NBA with the Los Angeles Lakers.

I'll always remember one of the first games I ever played for the Miami varsity. We had been practicing for several weeks and Mauer had scheduled a practice game with the Hamilton Business College. It was a Saturday night and it was New Year's Eve. You can see right then that New Year's didn't mean much in the Darrtown-Oxford area or we wouldn't have been playing basketball against a business college.

We'd gone home for the Christmas holidays but came back two days after Christmas to resume workouts—a short vacation, but when you play college basketball you never get much of a holiday season.

I had played some games earlier in Withrow Court (then the Miami fieldhouse) two years before as a freshman. I don't think any of us knew much about Hamilton Business College although some of the team had played in leagues around the area. By the half we were leading 42–6. When it was over it was 77–10, and Mauer used every man on the squad. Hamilton scored only one basket the whole game.

I don't think we learned much but it sure bolstered our ego. We thought we were pretty good until Mauer let the air out of our balloon. He told us they had lost to one of the rural high schools in the area before the holidays.

Usually Mauer played eight to ten men a game if it was close. In the tough ones many times five of us would go the distance.

That Hamilton Business College game might have been put on the schedule to give us a little confidence. One of our early games in December was down at Lafayette against Purdue, a mighty Big Ten power coached by Ward (Piggy) Lambert.

Now Purdue was pretty good, and big. They gave us a 48–24

lacing. It was their third win in a row and most of the experts predicted they'd repeat as Big Ten champions. All I remember is that we got eight field goals and eight free throws and were never in the game. I ended up as our second leading scorer with the magnificent total of five points. Purdue's leading scorer was Harry Kellar but he had only ten.

We weren't very big. Bob Dexter, one of our starting forwards from Lima, Ohio, was only 5-6 but he was quick and great on the break. At 5-8 Frank Vernotzy, our other regular foward, wasn't much bigger but he could also move well. I jumped center but John Anthony, who was just a shade taller than I, played the post on offense. He was the only out-of-stater on the team, coming from Whiting, Indiana.

Several fellows played guard alongside me—Warren Ott and Waite Bacon were two of them—but Warren Ott, who was about my size, usually started with me.

While Purdue had no trouble against us, when we went up against Indiana early in January of 1933 at Withrow Court, we must have gotten over a little bit of our fright against a Big Ten team because we played good ball. We led most of the game— never by much, but we led. John Anthony, working at center, led both teams in scoring 13 points.

Ralph Kirk, whom Mauer had kept out of the Purdue and Hanover games because of an eye injury, started with me at guard. Our two little forwards—Dexter and Vernotzy—drove Indiana crazy. They were so quick and scooted in and out so much that our set offense worked real well, and we upset the Hoosiers, 33–29. I ended up with five points, which just about matched the others except for Anthony.

It was a big win for the Miami team and a great win for the university, as Indiana was always up there with Purdue vying for the Big Ten title. It was a win Mauer was proud of. He played only five men, and we were just as ready to go the final minute as the first, thanks to his conditioning program.

The game I remember most of all in my three years of basketball was against Ohio University. There was quite a bit of rivalry between the two schools, and they had scored about 60 or 70 points against us down at Athens. With the center jump rule in effect then that was a huge score and represented a real drubbing. We were pretty short of talent this year and Mauer had moved me to center for most of the games. Ohio's center was Beanier Berens, about 6'5" and a big center then.

Johnny worked with me all week on how to play Berens, how to play alongside him to try and keep them from getting him the ball. When he did get the ball, I was to force him to the side, away from his favorite hook shot. It all worked out well. At one point we had a good lead, leaving the floor ahead at the half.

Withrow Court was packed with one of the largest crowds in history—they estimated 2,500—and when we won, 30–26, the place really broke loose with the noise.

Berens, who was the All-Ohio center that year, had been averaging 15 to 16 points a game. But I had the best defensive game of my life, and Berens got only 6 points on three field goals. I shut him out the second half. I was giving away considerable in height and I hadn't really played much at center previously except for the center jump.

I've always enjoyed basketball, especially in the years I've been in Los Angeles and have been able to watch Johnny Wooden's wonderful teams at UCLA. For years and years people kept telling me that I had played against John in those games Miami had with Purdue. That was a long time ago, and I usually knew who I was going to play against by number rather than name, so I'd just nod my head. Finally, after a number of writers kept asking me about it we called Johnny Mauer down in Knoxville where he is retired.

The Coach looked it up. Wooden graduated from Purdue in the summer of 1932. I know I didn't reenter Miami until that fall. So Wooden and Alston never quite met on the basketball floor, and from what I've read about John Wooden as a player, it was probably a good thing for me.

Miami tried to help us as much as possible to stay in school by locating part-time jobs for us when there were any to be had. I used to work on the paint gang during the off-seasons and if there was work in the summers. We painted dormitories inside and out. The rooms were small and the turpentine-base paints really got to you. Painting the ceilings in little closets was awful. Your eyes would water until you couldn't see; it bothered you to breathe; and your hands were always stinging.

The scariest assignment was painting in the big auditoriums

33

or assembly halls where you had to get up on the scaffolding formed by big A-frame ladders. The only thing between you and the floor was a 12-inch plank, ten or twelve feet long. It was pretty wobbly, especially with someone else working at the other end, and it was no fun reaching up to paint a ceiling. There were only three of us on the whole paint gang that would do it.

One year we repainted the whole football stadium. We'd go along with a scraper, removing all the loose paint and cleaning up the seat surfaces before applying the new coat. We were sure we'd never get done.

The paint gang always went to work almost the next day after school closed in late May or early June. Baseball ended then too, of course, so overnight I would go from my favorite pastime to a most boring task.

I don't think there was ever any doubt in Frank Wilton's mind about my love for baseball. If I wasn't the first one on the practice field each day, I was close to it. About the only thing that would detain me was a late lab, and even then I'd figure out some way to slip off a bit early to get out on the field.

Our college baseball season was always too brief for me. The East and Midwest have a considerable weather factor to contend with, compared to California, Florida, and the Southwest generally. The college seasons there are almost as long as some of the minor leagues used to be. Our season may have been only about a dozen league games and a half-dozen practice games. Even then sometimes we might be hit by a real cold spell or a few snow flurries.

One thing I will say for baseball at Miami—the quality of play was pretty good, and we had good facilities and good equipment.

A lot of the basketball team played baseball. One year there were six or seven of us on the team. I played third base my first year on the varsity and then shortstop two years. I wasn't a bad hitter, as I recall. I believe I was over .300 every year, and when you only play a few games that's not bad. I came to Miami as a pitcher, but pitchers didn't get to hit enough so I moved into the infield. I did pitch a few games, especially if we had a doubleheader.

Dad used to go to most of the baseball games if he was on

the right shift at Ford. Most of our games were in Ohio and not too long a drive.

About the third year at Miami I sold the Model T for either five or ten dollars. Dad helped me find a Model A roadster to replace it. I went for those open, soft-top jobs. Also, with the Model A having a rumble seat, I could drive two or three players to ball games around the area.

I was playing a little sandlot baseball from time to time for various teams—the Baldwins from Hamilton, among others. Weeb Ewbank, who later became Miami football coach, at one time was centerfielder for the Baldwins while I was shortstop. He was coaching in Oxford—football, basketball and baseball, as I recall—and playing baseball on the side.

That was probably the best town team I ever played on. We were all pretty good and a few of the semipros (and I assume Ewbank was in that group) were paid a little for each game. I didn't get anything except my expenses.

One thing all this did for me was to make my ability known to scouts. True, there weren't a great many of them coming around to Miami baseball games, but there were a lot more than ever found their way to a Milford Township High School game.

I suppose in the three years I played varsity baseball at Miami for Frank Wilton ten or fifteen scouts in all came to our games. But one of them counted. He was around quite a bit my senior year when we went down to the wire for the Buckeye Conference championship only to falter in the final game. We lost it to the University of Cincinnati, 8–6, due to six errors, and finished in second place behind Marshall College.

My degree was in hand a few days later. Now I'd see what was going to come of my hopes for a baseball career.

8

THE BASEBALL scouts weren't exactly banging on my door every day or two those last days at Miami. But I kept up my hopes during finals. There was a brief spark when I was in Withrow Court taking Coach Rider's exam in the theory of teaching track and field.

During the exam Coach Rider called me up to the desk and said he'd had a message that there was someone outside to see me. It turned out to be the superintendent from New Madison, who wanted to talk to me about teaching and coaching in the fall. Stepping out into the hall, I was introduced to Harold H. Cook. He was young for a superintendent, not more than three or four years older than I. He offered me $1,350 for the nine-month school year to come to New Madison, a little town about fifty miles due north of Darrtown and at that time just a little larger. That doesn't seem like much now. But it was a bird in hand and there was nothing in the bush that I could see, so I took it. We shook hands on the agreement and I went back to my exam. Mr. Cook promised he would mail me a contract as soon as he got home. I had it signed and back in his hands before graduation.

Following Miami's commencement ceremonies I immediately started helping Dad finish up his new house in Darrtown. It was still tough to find jobs in June of 1935.

The next day there was a knock at the door. When I answered it there stood Frank Rickey, the younger brother of Branch Rickey, who was then the general manager of the St. Louis Cardinals, the power in the National League.

Frank had seen me in a couple of Miami's games. I'd played short in one and pitched in another. After a few pleasantries we

36

got down to the nub of things. Did I want to play pro baseball? What a question to ask! I'd dreamed about that since I was old enough to throw that little rubber ball against the brick smokehouse out on our first farm. I explained to Frank that I had signed a teaching contract but that the job didn't start until September. He told me the minor league season would be over around Labor Day, which would give me plenty of time to get home.

I hadn't had any other offers, really. Oh, once the Cincinnati Reds invited me down to work out and I went. But it rained so they didn't see me. If anyone *had* offered me a contract along the way I'd have signed then and there.

I figured that if Branch Rickey's brother felt I was good enough for him to come all the way from St. Louis to Darrtown to sign me, I sure better sign and quick. He offered me a minor league contract at $125 a month. That was $25 more than the average, he said. I didn't ask anything else; I just reached for the pen.

Frank told me to get to St. Louis as soon as I could, preferably in a couple of days, and they would assign me to a club then. I don't remember what Dad said but I could see by the gleam in his eye that everything was OK. He never got a shot at baseball but his boy was going to. I know that my part of the paint job ended right then.

I'd signed June 19, 1935, and the next day, as I recall, Lela drove me to Richmond, Indiana, where I boarded a bus for St. Louis. I don't know exactly how many miles it is to St. Louis but I thought we'd never get across Indiana and Illinois. It was hot. Even with the windows open and the wind blowing in the bus was stifling. Air conditioning on buses, of course, was unheard of then. When we finally pulled into the terminal in St. Louis the second night, I was beat.

Frank Rickey had told me to check into the YMCA downtown. The next morning early I hiked over to the Cardinals' office. They had barely opened and I had to wait for Frank to show up. I waited around St. Louis for a week, going up to Rickey's office every morning to see if they had a place for me.

Finally one day Branch Rickey called me into his office and told me I was being assigned to Greenwood, Mississippi. That was a Class C league, then known as the East Dixie League.

Clay Hopper was the playing manager for Greenwood. Eddie Dyer, then a scout for the Cards and later their manager, drove me to Greenwood.

As I recall he had a roadster similar to the one I left with Lela in Darrtown. They'd told me Greenwood wasn't as far from St. Louis as Cincinnati was, but I thought we were never going to make it. We drove all one day and all that night. I can't remember that we stayed overnight anywhere but we must have. It seemed like it was a continuous trip. I do know we got to Greenwood, which is a little above the middle of Mississippi, around noon-time.

We didn't even find a hotel but went right to the park. Now Greenwood, Mississippi, in the tail end of June is a broiler. It was so hot games didn't start until 3 P.M. in hopes of avoiding the scorching temperature of midday.

Hopper penciled me in at shortstop that first game. He played the outfield. Although I had played short all through college and liked it, Hopper evidently didn't like the amount of ground I covered. The next day he put me at third base and I played third the rest of the season.

I hit pretty well that year, ending up with a .326 average in an 82-game season. I had only one home run my first year—a ride to dead centerfield with the wind blowing out in the Greenwood park. It was tough to hit home runs there. That park was big. The fences were way out there, and you really needed the wind to carry the ball out. I ended up with 104 hits, 25 doubles, 11 triples, and 46 runs batted in.

I found a rooming house to live in at Greenwood in a few days. After I had been there about a month I managed to save forty bucks some way. I decided I wanted to have Lela come down, so I bought a forty-dollar money order and sent it to her. We didn't call much then, mainly because we had no telephone at home.

I didn't hear from her and didn't hear from her. Finally I found out why. I had addressed the envelope to Oxford, Oxford, instead of Oxford, Ohio.

Because of my error she was about two weeks late getting to Greenwood. But the money finally did get there, and she took the Greyhound bus down and spent a two-week home stand with me.

The way the minor leagues were set up in those days I'd gotten onto a club that was up around what we now call Class A. It was a bus league and it seemed like it took forever to get around. More often than not the weather was miserable. One park in the league had lights so we played nights there, but the rest of the time it was day ball, with darn little breeze and plenty of heat. You never had a problem perspiring. Sometimes our uniforms were pretty rank.

I don't recall exactly how much meal money we got, but I'll guarantee it was under two dollars and probably more like a dollar and a quarter. You could get enough to eat for that money because nickel bread was around and a fifty-cent meal was a big one.

By the time Labor Day rolled around I was kind of glad to head for the bus stop in Greenwood so I could get back up to Ohio and teaching at New Madison. It didn't seem quite as long going home. I'll admit that I was a little homesick that season even though I loved baseball and all it meant. You can't spend all your life within ten or fifteen miles of one place and not miss it when you suddenly take off for three months.

I hadn't known what to expect going into pro ball, and it was the same with teaching. Luckily Lela and I had a few days around Darrtown before we had to head up Highway 127 for New Madison.

We must have looked like some gypsies as we pulled out of Darrtown in our Model A. We had things stacked everywhere —everything we owned. When we got to New Madison we were pretty fortunate to find a small house that rented for about ten dollars a month.

Each of our folks had given us a little furniture, and we bought some other things at a very reasonable price from the people who were just leaving the house. We were paying on the Model A, probably another ten dollars, and we'd splurged and bought a little table radio on time. That was costing us three dollars a month.

We got paid once a month—$135. There was no withholding, no insurance, no deductions then of any kind, so it was a full $135.

Every teacher's first assignment is a bit harrowing, I suppose. I had no idea what was going on as I started, but soon I realized that the kids wanted to learn, even the ones who didn't give any outward signs of it.

Kids always want to test a new teacher but I think I had a little more going for me than most. All of them—at least the boys—knew I had played pro baseball that summer and they were a little bit in awe over that. In addition, if there were any bullies in the classes, they seemed to think twice about challenging anybody my size.

I taught general science, physical education, and industrial arts. In addition I coached basketball every year but baseball the first year only. After that I left early for spring training.

We had a pretty good basketball season that first year for New Madison. After it was over the town threw a big dinner for the squad. Nearly everyone turned out to honor that basketball team. High school teams had a lot of community support then. There wasn't the competition of radio or television. Baseball season was brief and not as good that year because of so much rainy weather.

Another enjoyable thing about teaching—besides the association with the young kids—was the fact the faculty was comparatively young also.

Even though it was a small school district it was a group of fun people. Harold Cook, the superintendent, liked his golf and we'd slip away some afternoons for a game. Playing over at Richmond, Indiana, nearly twenty miles away, we had to hustle to get 18 in before dark.

One year just before the Christmas holidays we thought it would be appropriate to give the Ag teacher, a fellow named Woods, a practical present. I knew an old farmer who raised goats. One of them was getting a little too old to be much good and we bought him for little or nothing.

Cook and I went out in the roadster one afternoon while Woods was still teaching, loaded the goat in the rumble seat and hauled him back to Woods's house. We put a big ribbon around his neck and staked him out by the garage. Woods didn't know where it came from for quite a while. One day it butted his wife—knocked her down and sprained her ankle. That blew our cover and Woods had to get rid of the goat.

The music teacher, Forrest Hale, who was a fastidious guy, was very particular about his classroom and very strict with the band instruments and all his other music paraphernalia. He had a brand new music room, soundproofed, with the latest equipment. When I would leave my classroom to go to my mechanical drawing lab I'd have to pass his room. Every time I looked in all the chairs were in perfect lines, the desk was always clean, the drawers closed tightly and the blackboard spotless.

The first couple of days after noticing that, I'd push one or two chairs out of line when I'd go by. The next day I'd go over to the other side and move three or four. Every day I'd see him come in and straighten things back up, shaking his head.

I kept that up for about a week, making it a little messier each day. Then I'd turn some books around on his desk or pull out his desk drawers and reverse his own chair.

Every day he was getting tougher with the kids passing by in the hall, charging them with disrupting his classroom. Finally old Forrest Hale started getting on the kids in his class and the band pretty hard. I didn't want any of them in real trouble so I told him I didn't realize he wanted things in such neat order or I wouldn't have done it.

We're still pretty good friends. I hear from him every once in a while. He lives up near Toledo and once in a while will come down to one of our games in Cincinnati.

I really enjoyed my six years teaching at New Madison. It was a fine, young faculty and Harold Cook was a good administrator, easy to get along with yet able to maintain good staff discipline.

I'll never forget one afternoon when we'd skipped to play golf. We were over at the course in Richmond and he'd hit down into a thicket of trees. He was trying to figure out how to get out of that clutter. He rapped the ball a good lick and it took off like a shot, only instead of heading for the fairway it slammed into a tree. Back it came about twice as fast and hit him right between the eyes. It knocked him down but not out. I was real worried for a while.

All of us at New Madison were pretty athletically inclined, not that we were all stars, but we liked to play. In the winter we used to play some pickup basketball. Once in a while we might play the varsity to help raise a few dollars for something the school needed. Cook played and so did a fellow named Harry Moore, who really liked basketball.

There was also a little semipro basketball around and I'd play when I could. Sometimes the competition wasn't too good, but it was good exercise and we all had a lot of fun. In those days on the center jump you could tip the ball back to yourself. I'd tip it forward, run around the opposing center on a fast break and lay it in.

Teaching and the life associated with it gave me a lot of satisfaction. But baseball was always looming ahead. And as basketball season drew toward a close, I'd start throwing in the gym with the kids to get my arm in shape, take laps to keep my legs trim and scrimmage with them whenever it fit in.

By the end of my first year in late May of 1936 I was ready for another year with the Cardinals' chain.

9

FOR THE 1936 season St. Louis had assigned me to Huntington, West Virginia. That club was in a Class C league known as the Middle Atlantic League.

I looked forward to going to Huntington because it was familiar ground. Miami had played Marshall University in League Field, which was also the home park of the Huntington club, and I'd always hit well there. Getting to spend a season there was something I thought I was going to enjoy.

When I arrived in Huntington (a little late because of staying at school for the end of the kids' baseball season) Benny Borgmann, who was the manager, was back home because of the illness of his son, so I played second base. As soon as he returned he moved me to left field. I played there for quite a few games and enjoyed it. I had a strong arm and pretty accurate from my years of pitching. Some of the runners tried to take some liberties with me but after I'd cut down a few that ended.

So did my outfield career. Borgmann had problems at first base. One day he tossed me a first baseman's mitt and told me to take over. I hadn't played first enough to talk about in all my years but this move started something. Ultimately 99 percent of my career was at first, where I could move around pretty well and dig the ball out of the dirt. At 6-2 they had to fire pretty high to go over my head.

Borgmann was a patient man who knew his baseball and worked real hard with me to learn first. Since he was at second, right beside me, helped me adjust to playing the position, moving me in or out on various hitters and teaching me the small things you need to survive at first.

While Borgmann played second we had a youngster just coming into baseball who could sure cover the ground. He had a great arm too, although he sent me scurrying for a lot of balls. I remember he fired quite a few that even I couldn't get up there to grab, but baseball will long remember him as one of the greatest shortstops the Cardinals ever had. His name was Martin Marion, and he has to be up there with the great shortstops of all time. We called him Slats. He was real long-legged, could move all over, and any ball even close to him was his. Borgmann, being a second baseman, really appreciated his talents. Three or four years later Slats went up to the Cards, where he was a standout for years.

Marty may have been skinny as a rail, but he was about the only one off that club that made it to the big leagues and became what we call today a "super star."

It's difficult for a lot of ball players to realize that back in those days there were many, many more minor leagues than today. The ladder began with Class D and the rungs went up through the alphabet from C to B, A, AA, AAA and finally the big leagues. You almost had to serve a three to five-year apprenticeship before you'd even get a good trial in the majors.

Leagues literally covered the country whereas today baseball is confined to the large cities. Most of the famous names in minor league baseball cities have long been without teams. Back in 1936 the Cards probably had twenty farm clubs. Same way with the Dodgers. Today we have five clubs: Albuquerque, New Mexico, in the Pacific Coast League, which is triple A; Waterbury, Connecticut, in the Eastern League (AA); Lodi in the

California League (A); Danville, Illinois in the Mid-West League (A); and Bellingham, Washington, in the Northwest League (A).

An "A" league is the lowest classification in baseball today. Back when I was in Huntington that was three steps up the ladder. I think baseball lost a great deal when it gave up the expansive coverage it formerly had. It was a great learning experience, I can tell you that: You learned a lot about the geography of the United States traveling all over the country to play ball. And you met wonderful people. Other interesting things happened, too, like an experience I had in Huntington. Back then, minor league affiliates like Huntington had an agreement with the local sporting goods store to supply equipment and bill the club or perhaps the parent club—in this case the Cardinals.

Late one afternoon I went down to the sporting goods store to get a couple of bats. The fellow that owned the place showed me the stairs down to the basement where they stored the bats. I went on down and started going through them, testing how they felt, maybe swing through a time or two. How long it took I'm not sure but I finally picked out two that felt good to me and headed back up the stairs.

When I got to the top I went to open the door into the store. It was locked. I banged on it and no one answered. I banged again. No answer. I figured maybe they were up in the front and couldn't hear, so I really beat on it and yelled to have them let me out. Still no answer.

Now it was obvious. I was locked in. They'd forgotten about me and taken off for home. And we had a ball game coming up. There was no phone down there, of course, and there was no budging the door at the head of the stairs. There was no window in the basement; only a small crawl door with all kinds of bolts on the inside.

If some cop sees me crawling out of that space I'll end up in jail, I told myself. But I undid all the bolts, climbed out, throwing my two bats out ahead of me, and went around to the front of the store trying to find the owner.

There was no one in sight so I headed for the park. It was probably the only time in my career that I was ever late to the park. I told Benny Borgmann what had happened and he said he would get in touch with the owner so he could go back down to the store and lock up. I had pushed the little door closed but it wasn't locked.

At Huntington I had one of the best years of my career. I played in 120 games and went to bat 482 times. I hit .326, which was right up there for the league lead, and I led the Middle Atlantic in home runs at 35. Of my 157 hits, 16 were doubles and 8 triples. I scored 89 runs, drove in 114, and made only 22 errors for a .978 field percentage.

Now that's a long time ago, but there does appear to be a little discrepancy between my official record in *The Sporting News* and a clipping from the *Huntington Herald Dispatch* of September 2, 1936. On that day a writer named Wells Gaynor wrote that the night before I had hit my 36th home run and with seven more games to go had a shot at the league record of 38 set by Frank Welch, who was managing Beckley back in 1931.

The record book shows I hit 35 for the year and the clipping says 36. I don't know. The reason I even have that article is that was the day the Red Birds (as Huntington was known) sold my contract to the St. Louis Cardinals. Harry Hutton, who was president of Huntington, and Sam Politano, the business manager, made the sale to the Cards for what the paper said was an "undisclosed sum."

When Borgmann told me about it I was really jubilant. I was to report to the Cards at the close of the Middle Atlantic League which had about another week to run. My sale also created a problem: I was supposed to be in New Madison to teach in ten days. But that was the kind of a problem I liked.

I sent a telegram to Harold Cook explaining my sale and when I would report. When the leave I requested was granted, I called Darrtown and talked to everyone on the phone at the general store. I just couldn't wait for a letter to get home to tell everyone I'd be finishing out the National League season under Frankie Frisch.

It was unusual then for a major league club to dip down to the Class C league for a player. I guess I impressed Branch Rickey, Jr., who did a lot of scouting in the minor leagues for his father. He must have thought I was the best hitter he ever saw because every time he'd come in the park I would hit a home run or two or have a good day at bat with three or four hits.

One of the first times he had ever seen me play was the year before in Greenwood. Late in the game we needed a run to keep it alive. I had struck out three times before, and the count was 3 and 0 on me when Clay Hopper gave me the sign to hit away if it was my pitch. It was one I liked and I rapped it out to drive in the winning run. Rickey called me over after the game and asked: "What was the most important thing in the game today?"

I picked out a couple of key plays someone made. He disagreed. "The most important thing was that you didn't let the previous three strikeouts upset you. You went up there and picked out your pitch on a 3 and 0 count to drive in the run that counted most."

No doubt he remembered that during his swings through Huntington. I had really had a good season but, still and all, it was Class C ball and there were a lot of steps between there and the major leagues.

I remember the day in Huntington when they hoisted the 1935 pennant at League Field. We'd been playing for about two months or so and this particular night we were meeting the Johnstown (Pennsylvania) Johnnies.

A fellow named Harry (Red) Swain was pitching for Johnstown and in the first inning—just after they had run the pennant flag on the pole in centerfield—I hit a home run off him. Dick Lang, a Californian from Long Beach, was on base and he scored ahead of me. It was my twenty-first home run and we beat the Johnnies, 12–2.

Branch Rickey, Jr., might have been there that night because it was a big celebration—I can't recall. He was in and out during the season probably seeing us three or four times, maybe more. But out of all his swings he saw something he liked, and I sure liked the word that I was going up to the Cardinals.

It was a dream come true.

10

WHEN HUNTINGTON closed the Middle Atlantic League season the business manager or somebody gave me a railroad ticket to New York City and expense money to continue on to Boston. I was supposed to pick up the Cardinals there as they opened a series with the Braves.

I had been on a train only a few times in my life. That was back when I was a kid and my grandmother used to take me from Somerville down to Hamilton to see the Butler County Fair.

In those days, with railroads crisscrossing the state it was nothing for folks to board a train to ride eight or ten miles to a city. Buses hadn't taken over then. I hadn't been any further than that so when I got on the car to go to New York it was quite a thrill.

I'd heard of New York City, of course, and the Giants and the Yankees and the Dodgers, but I didn't think I'd ever go there. I sure didn't dream about going there as a baseball player.

Huntington was due west of Charleston—right on the border of Ohio—and the train ride to New York took several hours. I can't remember if I was aboard overnight but it definitely was the first time I'd been on a train with a dining car. I'll never forget the waiter bringing me the finger bowl and wondering what I was supposed to do with that. When I saw another diner dip his fingers in, I dipped mine too.

Coming into New York and Grand Central Station I'll never forget. I had an old suitcase about the size of today's cardboard soft drink container. I'd traveled all over the Middle Atlantic League for a full season with it.

47

As I was going through that huge train station, gawking around at the people and up at those high ceilings, I ran into some lady. The collision knocked me one way and my suitcase the other. The suitcase hit the floor, broke open at one end, and scattered all my clothes and belongings across the floor of Grand Central.

I don't remember if it was rush hour or not. All I know is that there seemed to be hundreds and hundreds of people all racing in a different direction. And here I was on my hands and knees trying to pick up my shirts and shorts and shaving gear— everything I owned—and to keep from being trampled by those rushing by.

Finally I had them all gathered together in what was left of my suitcase. I did my best to hold the whole business under my arm, wondering at the same time where I could find a paper bag or something to get me to Boston. Someone must have told me there was a store out in front of Grand Central that sold luggage. I think I had only twenty dollars or so when I left Huntington, but I spent some of it for another cardboard suitcase. After I repacked my things at the store, I tossed the old suitcase in the trash.

Now I had to tackle the problem of how to get to Boston. Finally I found a bus station and someone pointed me to the right bus. When I arrived at the Kenmore Hotel in Boston where the club was staying, they were already playing and it was too late for me to try and make the game.

I registered, and they were expecting me. The clerk at the desk told me that I could go eat in the dining room if I was hungry. All the ball players signed their checks. You can bet I was hungry after being on a bus several hours. Besides, I had darn little money left after buying a suitcase and a bus ticket to Boston.

I went in the dining room and some dude in a monkey suit —a tuxedo—seated me. One look at the menu convinced me I was in for a hard time. I had never heard of half the things and couldn't pronounce most of the words.

In Huntington we'd eaten in hamburger joints. We had $1.25 a day meal money and I didn't see anything on this menu for that little. Finally I decided on some clams. I'd always heard

Boston was famous for them. When they brought them out I wasn't sure just how you were supposed to eat them, but I managed all right.

As I remember, I didn't go to my room. I just sat around the lobby watching the people come and go while I waited for the team to get back from the park. I didn't want to miss them.

This was the era of the famous Gashouse Gang. Many of baseball's great figures were on the club. Frankie Frisch, the manager, I'd heard about in training camp as a real tough bird. He'd led the Cards to the World Series two years before, beating the Tigers in seven games with Mickey Cochrane, Charley Gehringer, Goose Goslin, Hank Greenberg, Schoolboy Rowe, Tommy Bridges and all that gang.

Frisch, who was still a playing manager in 1936, appearing in 93 games, won the seventh game of the 1934 series with a key double in third inning. That's the inning St. Louis scored seven runs.

This was the Cardinal club that had Pepper Martin, Rip Collins, Johnny Mize, Joe Medwick, Leo Durocher and the Deans—Dizzy and Paul. They were always up to something, I remember, and Pepper Martin was the ringleader.

You can imagine how I felt waiting in Boston for the bus to bring in all these people who up to now had been just famous names. Here I was, a farm boy from Ohio, completely lost in my meanderings in two of the largest cities in the East.

But I managed all right, thanks to another Ohio farm product named Jess Haines. His name won't mean much to modern-day baseball fans, but Pop, as most of the players called him, pitched for the Cards for eighteen years. He was pretty much a relief pitcher in 1936 although he had a 7–5 record.

Pop deserved his name. The records show he was 43 years old then, having been born in Clayton, Ohio, in 1893. He kind of took me under his wing, although I roomed with Don Gutteridge. Don, who came up at the same time I did, stuck around for twelve years in the major leagues, primarily as a second baseman.

Haines showed me what to do and how to do it. No matter what I asked he knew the answer. Most days he took me to and from the ball park. He was my buddy, more or less, but I am

49

sure it meant a lot more to me than it did to him. It's funny how you remember guys who do you a favor—especially in time of need, and, boy, I was in need.

He was still a big, old farmer up at Phillipsburg, which is a little west of Vandalia, where they have the great shoot every year. I don't think I realized that he had been in the big leagues since right after World War I. He pitched a no-hit game July 17, 1924, against Boston, and he was a 20-game winner two or three times. Altogether he was with the Cards from 1920 until he retired after the 1937 season. I'll never forget him or how generous he was to me.

Most of that September I spent on the bench. Before the games I pitched a lot of batting practice and took infield with the rest of the rookies who'd been brought up that year. I'd been brought up to play first, but with Rip Collins and Johnny Mize on hand, there wasn't much room for me. Fact is that Collins played most of the time in the outfield or pinch-hitting, with Mize, who was a rookie that year and hit .329, on first more often than not.

One afternoon after my batting practice pitching I was at third, just shagging balls and throwing them to first, when Joe Medwick tied into one. I leaped up over my head and back-handed the ball. I didn't think anything of it until he came around third after he had finished his turn and said: "What are you trying to do? Show me up?"

For the next two or three days whenever Medwick came up while I was pitching batting practice I'd reach back a little on the fast ball or pitch him down or away, being real careful not to give him anything good to hit.

As I said, you remember the good guys, the good things that have happened to you. You also remember the blasts you've taken from the stars.

While I loved every minute of that September with the Cardinals and the thrill of riding trains from city to city, I didn't get much of a chance to show if I could or couldn't play major league baseball.

One chance came when we were playing the Cubs in St. Louis in a game that had a bearing on third place for the two clubs. The Cards were behind. Frisch, I believe, had used Collins to pinch-hit, and Johnny Mize got thrown out of the game in a dispute with an umpire.

I went in to play first and didn't do too well. I made one put-out in the field and was charged with one error. My only time at bat in the major leagues came against Lon Warneke, one of the ace pitchers for the Cubs.

Warneke, a big but lean and lanky guy, could really whip that ball in there. I got hold of one of his fast balls and ripped it down the line, but it just eased wide of the foul pole. The next one he fired by me for a strike-out.

Lon had been a 20-game winner or right near there for five or six years and was one of the finest pitchers in baseball. Later he umpired in the National League, and I used to kid him a little about striking me out when we'd meet at home plate to exchange the batting cards.

Being struck out by Lon Warneke is about my only distinction as a player in the major leagues. I still say that one inning and one at bat isn't much of a test. But in those days, with hundreds and hundreds of players, that's what a lot of guys got. Some didn't even get that.

11

SPRING TRAINING of '37 in Florida was just another look for me before I was assigned to Rochester in the International League. I had hoped they'd give me a little closer one, but the Cards had picked up Dick Siebert from Brooklyn during the off season. With three first basemen now, there was little hope for Walt Alston. While I could play the outfield in the minors, I knew that my speed would never carry me through such an assignment in the big leagues.

Years later I learned from a Branch Rickey interview that the Cardinal organization had me tagged early on as not having the tools to cut it in the major leagues. But I was still young and eager and a believer in myself, and I stuck with the game I love.

Every year as I moved up a bit higher and a bit higher in baseball, greater problems were created for me as a teacher. I had to leave early each year for spring and report late every fall. That put a burden on the school district and especially the superintendent, Harold Cook, to find a substitute for me at both ends of the school year.

It was becoming more and more difficult for Cook. Teachers weren't too plentiful, and finally he told me I had to make a choice—New Madison or baseball.

At the time it wasn't too tough a decision. I was making almost as much playing baseball in the summer as teaching school. I don't think I ever made more than $2,000 as a teacher, and as I moved up in baseball my salary was getting a lot better.

Two schools made me offers shortly after that. The first, Eaton, would have been more money but would not have allowed me to miss any time. The second, Lewistown, worked out a compromise for me. They would let me report after baseball season closed and leave early for spring training.

Lela and I hated to leave the good friends we'd made in New Madison during the six years we were there. But we were grateful at the same time for the opportunity to stay with teaching in the off-season from baseball.

I have always enjoyed kids and young people. Being around them keeps you young, from getting set in your ways. And the high school kids I had in my classes were a joy to teach because they were always so eager to learn.

Again at Lewistown I was teaching subjects I enjoyed— mechanical drawing, biology, general science, woodshop and the like. On top of that I always coached basketball, and most of the players were in at least one of my classes. I never had much of a problem with discipline. We'd talk a little bit about basketball and then get down to the subject at hand. When we went to work they did a good job.

Once in a while I might have to sit on one of them, but not often. Most of them seemed to realize how important what they were learning would be when they had their own farms some day. Lewistown's agriculture teacher created problems for himself, however. He was always bragging about what a stern disciplinarian he was, that he was a judo expert and none of those big hayseed kids were going to get away with anything with him. Of course, some of those big kids acted pretty ornery in his classes, and he was always on them.

The ag class shared space in the woodshop, and I vividly remember the year they were building a hog house. They were in and out of the woodshop using tools and leaving things a mess.

They were about through with the project when one day just after the bell rang I began to hear a big commotion. The noise seemed to be out in the ag area, and I didn't pay much attention at first. Then I realized someone was yelling and pounding.

"Let me out, let me out. You let me out."

I didn't know what had happened, but soon I realized that the ag teacher was locked in somewhere. Glancing out a window, I could see that the kids must have gotten tired of his guff and nailed him in the hog house. I just said to myself, "If you're dumb enough to let those guys lock you in there I'm going to let you sit awhile."

I went on about my work as if I didn't hear a thing. Pretty soon the superintendent came by asking if I had seen the ag teacher.

"No, I haven't see him." I wasn't lying. I hadn't seen him. I just heard him.

The superintendent went out in the shop room and found him in the hog house. You know, those kids had taken twenty-five-penny nails and closeted him up good and tight. I had to take a big crow bar to break him out.

They had tricked him into coming inside by telling him they couldn't fit in the final piece of flooring. Once he was inside they closed and locked the door and nailed it shut. I enjoyed the episode as much as the kids.

All those years I taught school my love for hunting and shooting increased. Lewistown was very close to a good-sized lake—Indian Lake—and we took full advantage of it. Lela and I would often get up real early before classes and go duck hunting. About an hour before daylight we'd drive the three or four miles to the lake, get in a boat and row out to some cattails that served as a blind.

One very cold morning, we had sat and waited for quite a

long time without seeing any ducks. On the chance we might be missing some shots at a little pond behind our cover, I told Lela to wait in the boat and I'd walk back there. I'd done it a half dozen times before. It was swampy but solid enough. I was creeping over the cattails, moving as quietly as I could, when all of a sudden the bottom fell out under me and I found myself in half-frozen muddy water up over my waist. The only thing that kept me from going under was my gun, which had caught on some cattails.

Here I was a couple hundred feet from Lela, all alone and shivering cold. I didn't dare yell. If I did we both would get trapped. Finally using my gun and pulling on some cattails I managed to struggle back to the boat. Now I had to row a quarter of a mile, thoroughly chilled and with the temperature near freezing. I thought we'd never make the shore and the shelter of the car. By the time we did, my teeth were really chattering.

I spent a lot of hours during the school year either hunting or shooting, but I wasn't really in the same class with the men shooting skeet. All I had was a double-barreled Fox gun Dad had bought me when I was old enough to handle a shotgun.

It was a practical, all-around gun. The left barrel was full choke, the right barrel modified. I had used it mostly for hunting rabbits. After a few Sundays watching them shoot trap, I tried a few rounds myself. I got where I could break ten in a row pretty often.

All the rest were using trap guns. They were about four inches longer than mine and had really fancy decorated stocks. One Sunday when they were having a handicap tournament, I took the old double-barreled Fox out there. It cost ten dollars to enter and I wouldn't have been in it, but they didn't have enough shooters and asked me to fill out the squad. Contestants were to start by shooting 25 birds from 16 yards and then to move back according to the number broken. If you broke 24, for example, you'd move back to 24 yards, and so on. I got lucky. The first round I broke 25 straight from 16 yards.

On the next series, from 25 yards I broke the first 15 and missed the 16th, broke another and missed one about the nineteenth or twentieth. I ended up breaking 48 out of 50 to finish second.

That started me. I was hooked. A few years later I got my

first trap gun, and I spend a lot of leisure hours on the range these days.

Lewistown was my last teaching assignment. I'd become a playing manager in 1940 and this meant getting to spring training on time. That required me to leave school earlier than usual.

In my general science class while I was teaching at Lewistown, I had one student who really caught my eye, a cute little cheerleader for the basketball team. It was my daughter.

12

DORIS LA VERNE ALSTON had been born in Darrtown back when we didn't have too much and things weren't too bright for the future. I was still a college student at Miami and my baseball hopes were still a dream.

Dodie has made most of the stops along the way with me, from Greenwood, Mississippi, in 1936 on up to St. Paul and Montreal. Fortunately, most of her years in school were spent in New Madison and Lewistown. She was graduated from Lewistown High in 1948.

We both finished Lewistown together, she as a student and I as a teacher. When I moved up to St. Paul as manager in 1948 it was Triple A ball. Now there was no question of arriving late at spring training. Not only was there considerably more work to do in preparation for training, the season was much longer, with the possibility of being in the Little World Series.

I notified Superintendent Thrush after I'd been moved up to St. Paul that I would not return in the fall of 1948. That closed a fourteen-year teaching career that I cherished in many ways. I truly enjoyed being around the youngsters. You could bank on every day being different.

55

Most of the students I taught were going to get only a high school education, and most were going to be farmers. I tried to give them practical things in all my classes—general science, woodworking and mechanical drawing. In that way they'd know a little about soil; how to fix a wagon bed or make a door or build a chicken coop; and, if they were going to add on to their house, how to lay out a floor plan and make a lumber estimate.

Not many went on to college. In fact, I don't recall that a single one of the fellows who played basketball for me went beyond high school. But I think a lot of them have done real well in life.

When I quit teaching it stayed in the back of my mind that if I couldn't cut it in the high minors I could always return. That possibility ended a few years back when I became eligible for teachers' retirement at age sixty. Now I receive a little check every month for $37.15, so if anyone ever doubts I taught school I can pull out my retirement check stub and prove it.

And now what I want to do when I hang them up with the Dodgers is just to go home to Darrtown and do the little things I enjoy so much.

Baseball's been mighty good to me and I'd do it all over exactly the way I've done it. I might like to get more than one at-bat in the big leagues, but it's been a good life just the same.

After spring training in 1937, St. Louis had sent me up to Rochester, New York, in the American Association. Things were going along pretty good there when Branch Rickey called that I was being sent to Houston. Their first baseman had broken his leg and I was going to take his place.

The very day I got the word, Dad and Lela and Dodie had just arrived from Darrtown. They had driven the Model A all the way to Rochester and now we had to turn right around and head for Texas. Lela had just come from the grocery store when I got the call.

We were supposed to fly down. I'd never flown nor had Lela or Dodie. After a lot of tears, I finally called Rickey and asked if I couldn't drive down, going by Darrtown to drop Dad off. Mr. Rickey said it was OK so we left the next day.

It's quite a piece from Rochester, New York, to Houston, Texas, especially in a Model A. Somewhere in Arkansas, up in the mountains, we had car trouble and had to wait a day for a part to come from Little Rock or someplace.

As I recall, we were still two or three hundred miles from Houston when the engine got to knocking. In those days engine knocks were common but not always serious. We pulled into a garage in this little town and the mechanic said we had a rod gone. It was about 90° and the humidity was just about as high. We finally reached Houston either on or the day before the Fourth of July. And if we thought Arkansas was hot, it was nothing compared to Houston.

For the next five years I was in the Middle Atlantic League spending 1938 and part of 1939 at Portsmouth, Virginia, and the remainder with Columbus, Georgia, in the Sally League. Clay Hopper was the playing manager at Columbus and I had one of my best years, hitting .323 with 82 RBIs and 11 home runs.

Clay and I battled through the season for the club batting lead. He was ahead of me by two or three points when we came down to the last of the season with a doubleheader. In those final two games I'm not sure now whether I went six for seven or seven for eight, but it was something like that, and I ended up leading the club in hitting.

But back about 1938 I had realized when I went back to Portsmouth after a year at Houston and Rochester that I wasn't going to make it in baseball as a player. I had hit .246 at Rochester in 66 games and .212 in Houston in 65 games and never set the world on fire with my power, although I could still hit a long ball. I knew if I was going to stick around base-ball—which I wanted to do—it would have to be as a minor league manager or a coach.

When I got back to Portsmouth in '38, Benny Borgmann was managing. From then on I was always asking why he had done so and so, what his reason was for changing this pitcher, or any number of things. Several times I'd filled in as manager when the man had been kicked out of the game. I liked it. I liked the challenge of matching wits with the guy on the other club. So when after the 1939 season Mr. Rickey asked me to go back to Portsmouth and be a playing manager, I jumped at the chance.

We didn't set any worlds on fire that first year. We finished sixth but I led the league in home runs with 28 and hit .274.

In 1941 I began a two-year stand in Springfield, Ohio, which was also in the Middle Atlantic League. The first year we finished fourth and I led the league in runs at 88, home runs at 25, runs batted in, 102, and in assists with 86 and fielding at .989.

The following year at Springfield we were fifth but I had another good year playing, leading the league in home runs (12), runs batted in (90), hitting (.310), put-outs (1117), assists (106) and fielding (.990). We had some pretty good kids on the club: Herb Adams, Tom McNulty, Bob Collett, Joe Neidson, Gene Ciolek, Forest Rogers and Tom Ashbury, to name a few.

As I recall, it was with Springfield that I finally made $2,000 managing. In those days that was awfully good money. In fact, that was more than I was making teaching, which was a whole lot more work.

That winter World War II broke out. Like everyone else, I fully expected to be on my way in one branch of the service or another. But I flunked my physical. A college basketball injury to one knee wouldn't allow me to execute a squat that was required by the service.

With the war on, every club, especially in the minor leagues, was hard-pressed for manpower. We had come into Dayton with our pitching staff in bad shape, having just played a double-header, and we had a single game and another doubleheader coming up.

I was down to deciding whether to pitch a young kid with one day's rest or pitch myself. I hadn't pitched a game since college but I did throw batting practice almost every day. Dayton had a pretty good club and their scheduled pitcher was Nelson Potter. He was a good-sized right-hander who went on to the majors for a twelve-year career.

I decided it would be better to see what I could do than to risk the young guy's arm with a day's rest. So I started against Potter. I knew I could get the ball over the plate and not make too much of a farce out of things. As I moved along I felt fairly good. After a couple of innings I gained confidence and started to mix things up, changing speeds often and trying to hit spots on the corner of the plate.

We had to go into extra innings and I finally lost to Potter in ten innings, 2–1. The next morning when I woke up I could hardly raise my arm but I still felt pretty good. I had pitched ten innings in a pretty good Class A league against a pretty fine pitcher in Potter and didn't embarrass anyone.

The war was on full bore in 1943 when I was assigned to Rochester in the International League. I played in 115 games at first and third, but was not impressive, ending up with a .240 average.

Somewhere along the line in those war years I played against Bob Feller in a spring game. I don't remember what club I was with, but it might have been Rochester. I got a couple of hits off Feller, who was just as swift as they always claimed.

Now don't misunderstand me. I was no expert at hitting fast balls and that's what Feller had in those days, a super fast ball. I was probably known as a fast-ball hitter, but I hit more home runs in my life off curve balls. A high curve ball, in my opinion, is one of the easiest pitches to hit, and minor league pitchers throw that pitch more often than major leaguers do.

I played thirteen years in the minors as a player and player-manager. The Dodgers researched my career batting average at .295. That wasn't bad, but I'm the first to admit that in the minor leagues you get a lot more mistake pitches to hit than you do in the majors. In some respects, however, a minor league pitcher is tougher on a batter because so many of them are wild and you'd better be loose up there. In the majors you know the pitcher is going to be in and around that plate pretty close, and that's an advantage to the batter.

For all of 1943 and thirteen games of 1944 I was with Rochester. I hurt my back sliding one day early in the 1944 season. It took a long time to come back, and finally the Cardinals gave me my outright release.

That was probably the darkest hour of my life. Mr. Rickey had left the Cardinals and moved to Brooklyn. I'd been around a long time in the Card organization and they no doubt figured I wasn't going to be much help to them in the future. Since I was hurt they released me.

I had returned to Darrtown prepared to stay in teaching. My baseball career appeared to be at an end. But one day the son of the man who ran the general store knocked on the door and said there was an urgent long distance call for me.

It wasn't too far to the store, a couple of blocks. I set a new record getting there. Mr. Rickey was on the phone. First thing he did was give me a good going over for not having a phone and told me to get one. Then he offered me the manager's job—really the playing manager's job—at Trenton in the Interstate League for the remainder of the season.

Both Branch Rickey and Branch Rickey, Jr., had seen me play a lot of games. They always liked me, I guess. I didn't cause them any problem. I played baseball, did my job, and took care of myself. I never smoked until after I was finished as a player.

Neither of the Rickeys could understand how I could hit so well and do things so well when they were around but couldn't keep that up all the time. Mr. Rickey must have seen something he liked about my managing because once he heard the Cards had released me he started trying to reach me.

It was several days before he had the Dodger operator try to find a store or something in Darrtown with a telephone. It didn't take them long to find the general store and me. It took me far less time to be on my way to Trenton.

As in most of the low minors, the Trenton manager did everything—manager, traveling secretary, trainer, grounds-keeper, the whole bit. You'd go out early in the afternoon and water down the infield so it would be a little smoother. You'd pitch batting practice. Hit infield and before every game take a damp cloth and rub the grass stains off the practice balls so you could use them in batting practice.

Nowadays players wouldn't even play pepper with the balls we used in batting practice. And what we use in batting practice today were game balls in Trenton. It was a Class B league and Trenton was one of the better cities located in New Jersey.

I spent the remainder of 1944 and all of 1945 with Trenton. We were sixth the first year and third the next. I was only in 52 games in '44 but I came to play after Mr. Rickey gave me a second chance in baseball. I hit .350, hit 9 home runs and drove in 48 runs. The next year I was in 126 games, had 14 homers, 93 RBIs and hit .313.

I have a couple of telegrams in one of my old scrapbooks in Darrtown. Every time I read one dated September 10, 1945, a lot of memories go by.

I THINK YOU DID A FINE JOB WITH TRENTON CLUB THIS YEAR. CONGRATULATIONS ON FINISHING IN THIRD PLACE.

60

BEST OF LUCK TO YOU AND ALL THE BOYS IN THE PLAYOFFS. BRANCH JR. TOLD ME TODAY THAT HE WANTED TO SEE YOU BEFORE YOU GO HOME SO TRY TO VISIT US WHEN YOU HAVE FINISHED.

BRANCH RICKEY SR.

It was great to be back in baseball. Now it was up to me to either succeed and climb up the managing ladder or devote myself entirely to teaching.

13

NASHUA, MAINE, of the New England League was a landmark in my life. I moved there in 1946 from Trenton, which was an affiliate of the Dodgers. The Nashua franchise was owned by Brooklyn, however, and totally funded by them. Going there marked the fact that I was slowly closing the book on my playing career.

I was in only fifty games at first base and was to appear in only two others in 1947 at Pueblo as a pinch hitter. From then on my baseball was from the bench.

Nashua had a Dodger in the front office, of course. His name: Emil J. Bavasi. With our association in 1946 began a relationship that grew closer and closer over the years.

Buzzie Bavasi, as everyone calls him, became one of my closest friends. Both of us ended up with the Dodgers for many years, Buzzie as general manager and in my opinion one of the finest there has ever been.

We were both relatively new to the Dodgers at Nashua. The club was loaded with what Brooklyn felt were bright young prospects. That was the year Jackie Robinson broke the color barrier by signing with the Dodgers and being assigned to Montreal.

At the same time, Mr. Rickey signed several other young blacks. Two of them—Roy Campanella and Don Newcombe —were assigned to Nashua. Now both were established stars in the Negro League. Campanella was a brilliant catcher who knew the intimate details of baseball exceedingly well. Newcombe, a big guy with a whip for an arm, could really fire that ball in there.

From time to time during the season, Campy and Newk heard some unkind remarks about their race. No one could help hearing them, they were so loud, but Campy was a quiet, level-headed man and he kept things under control.

There was no problem on our team. All the players accepted Campy and Newk from the outset. But why not—they were two fine men and very able baseball players, probably the two best on the roster. There was one time in Nashua when I protested a decision a bit too loud and got kicked out of the game. I named Campy manager without a minute's hesitation. He was the most knowledgeable player. He had more experience than any of the others and everyone respected him. He did a great job.

At the time there was one manager in the league who continually expressed his dislike for Campy and Newk in language no one should use. One night he got in a hassle with Bavasi over them. Since I was with Bavasi he objected to being confronted when the odds were two to one against him.

So the two of us marched right out behind him to the team bus and in the only language he could understand—harsh and quite profane—Buzzie told him off. Any number who cared to step forward were invited to come on out, but no one would back him up. That's the last we heard of him. Other than a few incidents like that we had no racial problems.

Campy did have a serious problem of his own creation. He could hit pretty long; as I recall he had 23 home runs or so for Nashua. Now one of the businessmen used to give a hundred baby chicks to anyone who hit a home run. Can you imagine what Campy would do with 2,300 chicks or so in Harlem? I don't think he ever went around to collect.

I never believed in bed checks or any of the other commonly used disciplinary tactics. I did have a curfew but I felt my players were men who cared enough about the game and their future to be in on time.

Buzzie Bavasi has been responsible for a lot of things in my life and one of them is golf. I hadn't played much golf when I got to Nashua, but Buzzie loved the game and played it all the time. Nashua had a nice golf course and Lela and I would often go out early in the morning to get in a round of play.

One day Buzzie and I went out to the country club with a couple of our players, Dick Malady and Larry Shepard, who later managed Pittsburgh. We were all pretty scatter-gunned but on the sixth hole Buzzie tied into one. It was a short hole but he hit the ball well and when we got up towards the green we couldn't find the ball.

We looked all over where we normally would find one of our balls—in the trap, off in the rough or buried in the fringe of the trap in that hanging high grass. I finally walked by the cup and I'll be darned if the ball wasn't in there lying at the bottom wedged against the pin.

Buzzie had a hole-in-one. Now that was his first, I guess, and he was mighty happy. In those days in Nashua you got a set of tires or a case of Scotch or something for an ace. So as we were walking into the clubhouse after the round, I turned to Shep and Dick and suggested to them that we never saw any hole-in-one.

"Sign my card, Walter," Buzzie asked me.

"Why?"

"For my hole-in-one."

"What hole-in-one? I never saw any hole-in-one. Did you, Dick? How about you, Larry? Did you see Bavasi get a hole-in-one?"

Buzzie was raging. Here his manager and two of his players were swearing they'd never seen a hole-in-one. Bavasi went to the telephone and called his wife, Evit.

Pretty soon Evit showed up in the clubhouse. We were having lunch. She had a book in her hand and she gave it to Buzzie. It was the release book of standard baseball forms they give any player when he has been released.

Needless to say, we all signed the card and Buzzie got his prize.

Another thing that happened that year at Nashua had longer-lasting consequences. We were playing the Giant farm club in the New England League. A fellow who later did some catching for New York named Sal Yvars hit a popup down the first base line, high and in about seven or eight feet toward the pitcher's mound.

I was calling for the ball and watching it and just about the time I caught it he ducked his shoulder into me and knocked me down. Now that was the last thing I was looking for. First of all, the fielder has the right of way, and, second, he had run way out of the base path and was automatically out.

I was knocked upside down and the first thing that hit the ground was the back of my neck. I couldn't wait to get over to first base. We met right there, swinging. I popped him a couple of times real good but the story that got out was that I knocked him out. That was an exaggeration. I didn't knock him out, and after two or three punches every one on both clubs was on the field.

But Yvars was an aggressive bulldog type guy who was no doubt really mad at himself for popping up. I do know that my neck bothered me for days and I missed most of the season. It's still a problem and I take a treatment two or three times a week the year around.

We finished second in the New England League and then went on to win the playoffs, beating Pawtucket three games to none and Lynn, Massachusetts, four games to two.

Mr. Rickey was quite pleased with our winning the pennant. That winter he asked me if I would take over Pueblo in the Class A Western League. I didn't even know where Pueblo was until he explained it was in Colorado near Denver.

"There won't be any difference in salary," he said, "but you'll be going from a Class B league to a Class A."

I felt he was testing me to see whether money or baseball came first.

"If it's a Class A league," I told him, "I'll take it."

"In that case," he added with a smile, "there'll be a little more money. Not much more, but a little more."

We had some real good talent. After finishing third in the standings, in the playoffs we beat Des Moines three games to one and then whipped Sioux City four games to two. Those two years were mighty important in my managing career. Back-to-back pennants in two different leagues spread nearly across the country seemed to impress Mr. Rickey as well as the other Dodger executives.

When I reported to the Brooklyn office at old Ebbets Field, Mr. Rickey greeted me warmly. After we went over the season, he offered me a big jump in salary and the manager's job at St. Paul.

That was a major turning point for me, taking me from A ball all the way to Triple A. That was just one step from the majors, and generally St. Paul was considered the Dodgers' number two triple A farm behind Montreal.

I went back to Darrtown in great spirits for the winter and another round of hunting and shooting with Dad and the fellows. It was quite a turnaround from two years before when I had come home from Rochester with my tail between my legs, figuring my unconditional release meant the end of my days in baseball.

14

WINTERS ALWAYS mean a lot to me. I'm back home with no pressures on my time. As long as I can remember I've gone hunting then. For all those years—until Dad died in May 1975 —more often than not it has been with him and some of the old guys around Darrtown.

Back in our days on the farm Dad helped supplement his farm income by hunting. After working all day on the farm Dad enjoyed coon and possum hunting at night. There was a pretty good market for hides, with a good-sized possum bringing about four dollars. Coon—and that's what we usually went looking for—could bring $18 to $20.

Coonskin coats were pretty popular then and it took a lot of coons to make a full-length coat for a man. You remember them? Jack Oakie always used to wear one in those college movies he made.

One particularly good night Dad and I came home with four coons. They were pretty large and brought about $20 or $25 apiece, a pretty good day's (or should I say, night's) work then. Of course, you might go weeks without getting one so it wasn't a very dependable source of income.

One of the fellows who's been hunting with us most of my life is Howard Cox. He's quite a guy, always playing jokes, but a fine fellow and a good shot.

I remember going out with him many times to shoot crows or chicken hawks, of which there were always a lot sitting on light poles or up in old dead trees. We'd go out riding around the back country dirt roads and Coxie would spot a hawk or a big fat crow maybe seventy-five or a hundred yards away.

He had a heavy .22 caliber rifle with scope sights on it, and this one day he knocked off a couple from an ungodly distance. Way over a hundred yards. I missed one about half that far.

Coxie gave me the horse laugh the rest of the day.

When I got home I told Dad what happened. The next day he and I went hunting for hawks. We must have driven twenty miles before we finally killed one. The temperature was about zero so we took the hawk and left it out overnight until it was frozen solid.

The following day we went out along one of our usual routes and wired that hawk up in a tree. A day later we got Coxie to go hawk hunting, and we led him around to the bird we had stashed. Coxie pumped enough shot into that bird to splatter him, but still he sat in the tree.

We ragged Coxie for hours as we rode around hunting. We never got off him. When we got home we dropped him at his house. Since we lived just across the street we watched his house out the window.

Coxie gave us enough time to get settled at home, but, sure enough, pretty soon we saw him backing out in his car. We followed right after, staying far enough behind him so he wouldn't recognize us. He drove out to where he'd missed that hawk. The bird was still in the tree, of course.

He took a couple more shots at the hawk from his car. Then

Left: Granddad Charlie and Grandma Hattie Neanover. Below: Emmons Alston and bride, Lenora Neanover Alston.

Walter Alston, age 5, ready to start school.

Farming the hard way. Walt and his dad await dog Shep's approval of their efforts.

Walt in Milford Township
High School baseball uniform.

Newlyweds Walt and Lela
Alston.

Faithful transportation. Walt stands beside
secondhand Model A Ford that got him back and
forth from Darrtown to Oxford, Ohio, and Miami
University, where he starred in basketball.

Left: Smokey Alston in first major league uniform. Above: Coach Alston (back row, center) with 1936 New Madison (Ohio) High School basketball team.

Above: In uniform for Huntington (W. Va.) Red Birds, 1936. Right: Second chance in baseball. In first two years with Dodger organization, Walt was player-manager for Trenton (N.J.) farm club.

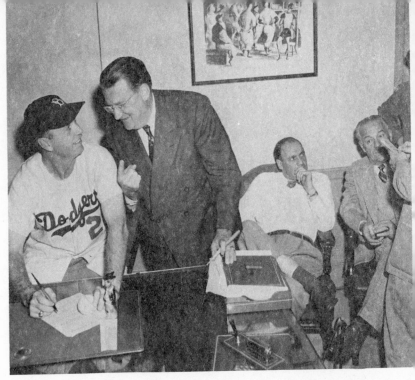

Walt Alston signs first of nearly a quarter of a century of one-year contracts with Dodgers. Owner Walter O'Malley holds up one finger to signify one year. Seated behind O'Malley are Buzzie Bavasi; (center) and Fresco Thompson.

Bursting their buttons with pride, uncle Stanley Alston (right) and father, Emmons Alston, relax with Smokey at home in Darrtown after signing.

Manager Alston. In first year with Brooklyn Dodgers, Walt handled third base coaching chores also. Photos at left (by Ernest Sisto, NYT Pictures) show different signs. Below, right: Hitting fungoes (New York Post photo by Barney Stein).

1955—a season to remember. Left to right, Manager Walt Alston, Captain
Pee Wee Reese, and outfielders Duke Snider and Carl Furillo spell out
with bats how it began, with ten consecutive Dodger wins. Below: In clubhouse, jubilant Alston, Walter O'Malley, and Reese celebrate Dodgers'
first World Series victory ever (New York Post photos by Barney Stein).

*The celebration continues. At home in Darrtown, Walt
(far left), beside his father, joins part of local parade.*

*1956—a year that almost was. Yankee manager Casey Stengel,
Dodger catcher Roy Campanella and manager Walter Alston await
start of World Series in Ebbets Field as Dodger owner Walter
O'Malley's distinguished guest, President Dwight Eisenhower,
throws out first ball (O'Malley is at Eisenhower's left in this* New
York Post *photo by Barney Stein).*

EARL (Red) BLAIK

GEORGE RIDER

PAUL BROWN

WALTER (Smokey) ALSTON

Miami University Hall of Fame

CHARTER MEMBERS

JAY COLVILLE

ARA PARSEGHIAN

JOHN PONT

WILBUR (Weeb) EWBANK

*Above:
One of Walter
Alston's most
cherished
honors.*

*Walt's parents,
Christmas 1966.*

he started down the fence row toward the hawk, stopping every so often to take another shot.

As Coxie crept closer so did we. After shooting a dozen rounds, he finally went right up where he could see he had been tricked.

He took the ribbing real well. Not long after, I got my sister, Dorothy, who's a pretty good artist, to draw me a hawk sitting up in this tree with all the bark skinned off from the missed shots. I gave that to Coxie.

Next to baseball I guess Dad enjoyed hunting and practical jokes best.

Dad's love for a little fun didn't keep him from being a fairly strict disciplinarian when we were growing up, but I don't think either Dorothy or I gave him and Mom much trouble. He never took me into the wood shed, and I am sure he never did her.

We were a close family, but when there is such a large age gap between children, as there was between Dorothy and me—twelve years—you don't have much in common until you get way up in your teens. And by then I was off playing baseball and not really around when she was in an age group where we'd have had similar interests.

On the other hand, Dad and I in many ways had a father-son relationship that was almost brother to brother. There weren't many things over the years we didn't do together and enjoy about the same.

Dorothy is Mrs. Kenneth Tolley now and lives on a farm about ten miles south of Darrtown and just west of Hamilton. We see a lot of one another during the off season. Her husband works at the Fisher Body plant in Hamilton and they live on a 140-acre farm that once belonged to his father. He's an executive with Fisher and doesn't do too much farming but still raises a few head of cattle.

They've got a young set of twins who come over a lot. They're aware of who their uncle is, but the big thing with them is to go for a ride on the back of my motorcycle. They get a big kick out of that despite the fact that they have ponies of their own.

In recent years since I've had motorcycles I often ride up through the park woods in the late fall just to look at the changing trees. It's truly beautiful there, but spectacular at this season.

A good part of my winters ever since I've been in baseball

have been spent out in the workshop Dad built. It's been added onto a time or two until today it's a pretty fine place to work.

It's primarily a woodshop although I have enough tools to handle a few other kinds of things. But as it was for Dad, woodworking is my first love. When it gets too cold or we have snow, I fire up the old pot belly stove out there and get to work.

There are power saws, joiners, planers, shapers, band saw, jig saw, drill press—just about anything you need to work in wood.

Over the years we've made a lot of things for the house, and lately I've made quite a few gun cabinets for friends. I probably can do one or two a winter, but that's about all. The last one I made out of black walnut, a wood that's not only pretty hard to come by now but costs like the devil. A real piece of furniture about six feet high and four or five feet wide, it was free standing and held seven guns.

The shop stands behind our home but was here long before we built. After Dad built his home on Apple Street, he bought four acres later on right across the street. On part of that acreage was an old barn. When he decided to build a shop he knocked out one side of the barn and built a block wall addition. A couple of years later, he added on another side and built the stable for our riding horses.

Back behind the barn there was a woods of thirty or forty acres that ran on both sides of a creek. I loved to ride those woods, and Dad often went with me. The owners didn't object and I've spent many an hour enjoying the quiet and solitude there.

We had a five-gaited horse named Dusty, a sorrel that had been raised for shows. Dusty was a beauty. She held her head so high, was one of those high steppers and had been trained so well. Like most thoroughbreds she was a bit high strung, gentle until you got up on her back, and then you'd better know what you were doing or you might be off her in a hurry. Dad thought a lot of her and rode her probably a greal deal more than I did.

Being a farmer, Dad was great with horses. He shoed all our horses. Only a time or two did a professional do them. Dad had all the tools—rasp, horseshoe pliers and pinchers—needed to shoe them.

76

Right after Dad expanded the barn into the shop he added a little shooting gallery where we could shoot .22 pistols at targets to keep our eye sharp. Behind the target there was a steel plate on a slant which diverted the bullets down into a pile of sand.

We spent many a winter night out in the shop working or shooting. In between there was a lot of baseball talk, especially in the later years, like when I moved up to St. Paul as manager.

15

NO ONE WAS MORE pleased by my becoming manager at St. Paul than Dad. He'd lived baseball as long as I can remember, and, when I was hired to be the Saints' manager in the Triple A American Association, we burned a lot of wood out in the shop stove working and talking.

Mel Jones, who became a very dear friend of mine over the years, was the one who told me that the job was mine. Back in 1948, Mel was the general manager of minor league operations for the Brooklyn Dodgers. He supervised all the personnel in the farm system.

St. Paul hadn't been doing too well for the Dodgers when I took over in 1948, and Mr. Rickey was the kind of a man who didn't like to see one of his prime Triple A franchises not doing well. Montreal, in the International League, was the lead Triple A club with St. Paul next. That meant when players were cut from the Dodgers at spring training, the first selections went to Montreal and the next came to me at St. Paul. One thing that differed in St. Paul from the lesser minor leagues was that I wasn't totally alone to run things. We had a trainer who, in addition to his duties taking care of the players' ailments, bumps and bruises, served as the traveling secretary. He took over a lot of the detail such as handling the hotel, handing out meal money to the players, checking on the buses and room assignments when we were on the road.

The American Association was mostly a train league. Of course, we didn't ride a train to Minneapolis since it was right next door, but the long hauls were by train—to places like Indianapolis, Columbus, even Milwaukee, which wasn't too far from St. Paul.

We traveled by sleepers and usually had a coach all to ourselves. The manager and the traveling secretary shared a compartment. All the regulars and the next day's starting pitcher had lower berths. The rookies and everyone else were in the uppers.

Actually, the uppers had more room, but they weren't as good because they didn't get as much air. With no air conditioning that was important in the summer. You could open the window in the lower and get what little air there was.

While Mr. Rickey always considered the International League and the American Association a step or two above the old Pacific Coast League, it was still a one-man operation from the manager's viewpoint. I always pitched batting practice, hit infield, and coached at third base.

You were a teaching manager then or you didn't survive. The major league club expected its farm hands to come up and know all the fundamentals. Nowadays you have to teach young players at the major league level. The farm system is too sparse to give them much of a chance to absorb all the fundamentals.

Back then you taught them. And the parent club was always calling some up on you. Then you had to go out and find someone yourself, work him in the morning and the afternoon to see if he could do the job. In the meantime, you were working some of the younger players on fundamentals during the same time. It was the only teaching time you had once you broke spring training and began to play.

St. Paul was a good baseball team. They drew well and there was a group of avid fans who loved the Saints and American Association baseball.

Sal Yvars, the catcher I'd had the fight with in Nashua, had been sent to Minneapolis by the Giants. About the first time we met them, he started in on me. That was pretty easy since I was coaching third and the Millers' dugout was right behind me. I took it for a bit, but then I just turned to him and said: "Just because you've got all your teammates with you, don't let that stop you from coming out of the dugout on your own if you want to." That was all there was to it. There wasn't even any conversation after that.

But there was one big redheaded fan in St. Paul I'll never forget. He came out almost every game and sat behind the big screen along the right field foul line near our dugout. We started to win pretty good that first year in 1948 and began to draw some good crowds.

This big guy sat behind that screen heckling me from the day we began. We'd been out on the road for a spell and had won something like eight out of ten. On one particular play where as third base coach nothing critical such as scoring a run or not depended on me, he really came down hard on me. I turned around so I could get a real good look at him. I knew who was doing it but I wanted to remember his face.

A day or two later I took Lela downtown to do some shopping. Since I'm not much on shopping, I went to a recreation center down the street to shoot some pool. We had agreed to meet in an hour and just about when the time was up I started walking towards the store.

About half a block from the store who should I see coming toward me but that big redhead. I tried to tell myself that the best thing to do would be to ignore the character. But the closer I got to him the madder I got. Then when he recognized me and spoke to me, everything came undone.

"Oh, yeah," I said, "I recognize you. You're the guy that's been doing all that screaming from behind the screen. I'll tell you what. I don't know for sure what you said but I think I know what you've said and I wonder if you've got the guts enough to repeat it right here."

"Oh," he said, "let's forget about it."

By now I was in gear. "No, we're not going to do that. If you can back up what your big mouth has been saying, now is the time to do it. Right now."

He tried to walk away from me. I turned around and walked right with him. Now I don't easily get mad, but when I do I'm usually beyond the point of control. He didn't stop so I just moved right in front of him, grabbed him by the shirt collar, and made him stop.

"Man," I was yelling pretty loud now, "you've been yelling at me all this time. You're going to wait until I get ready for you to go."

We were in downtown St. Paul. By now there was a pretty good crowd and I realized some of them knew who I was. Gradually I got control of myself, eased up on his shirt collar and said: "Well, if you don't have anything to say I'll wait and see what you do back of that screen."

You know, he still came to the games, but I never heard another word from him the remainder of my two years in St. Paul.

Things had been pretty bleak for St. Paul for some years. They hadn't won the pennant or the American Association playoffs since 1938.

Our first year in 1948 we finished third with an 86 and 68 record that made us eligible for the playoffs. We beat Indianapolis, who had finished first, four games to two, and then beat Columbus for the championship, four games to three. We lost the Little World Series to the Dodgers' International League farm club, Montreal, four games to one.

The Dodgers had a lot of clubs and a lot of players under contract in the huge farm system of those days. One pretty good little player was a shortstop named Buddy Hicks, who in '48 hit around .300.

I remember him in particular because the following spring Mr. Rickey wanted to sell Hicks. We were in a big league meeting with probably twenty-five to thirty people present. Mr. Rickey was talking about bringing Hicks up to Brooklyn and how he was going to hit that right field screen so well. Feeling that Hicks would not pull the ball that much, I finally spoke up. "Mr. Rickey," I said, "this boy has played for me all year and there were only two balls that he hit well all year to right field. They didn't reach our right field fence."

He talked about Hicks for another half hour and I refused to agree with him. Mr. Rickey was a great baseball man but I knew more about Hicks, I thought, than he did. He wasn't going to make me say something I didn't believe in. I felt that in the long run Mr. Rickey would respect me more for sticking up for what I thought was right than for being a yes man.

Hicks never made it up to the Dodgers but he did play briefly for the Detroit Tigers in 1956. That was his only season in the major leagues.

Baseball is a tough business, especially for a player. Most of the time you get one shot and if you don't make it that's it. There's no second time around. I feel that oftentimes is unfair but that's the way they've played the game since it began.

Our second year in St. Paul was highly successful. We won the pennant with 93 wins and 60 defeats, but we came close to blowing it and Mr. Rickey played a big part in the latter.

We had some fine young ball players along with some veterans with a long record of experience. Wayne Belardi was one of the bright youngsters at first base. Also a young black kid named Jim Pendleton. Then we had veterans like Danny Ozark, who coached for me for years and now manages the Phillies, and Eric Tipton. He was a famous halfback for Duke who played against Southern Cal in the Rose Bowl game they lost in the last seconds, 7–3.

Tipton, an outfielder, had been up in the major leagues with the A's and Cincinnati for seven years before being acquired by the Dodger organization. Ozark never made it to the major leagues as a player although he was a fine first baseman.

Rickey had brought Pendleton up from one of the lower farm clubs. Ozark, our first baseman, was hitting over .300 then. Pendleton and Wayne Belardi, a left-handed hitter who had a lot of power for a young guy, had joined St. Paul together. Belardi was a utility man with the Dodgers for a brief time during my first year as manager.

Pendleton was a young fellow who could really run as well as play centerfield. But Ozark was playing first for me and another seasoned veteran, Earl Naylor, was in center.

We had a six-game lead in the American Association with nine games to play when Rickey came in to see a Sunday doubleheader. Things were going great. We were clicking along and figured to lock up the pennant in a few more games. But Belardi and Pendleton weren't playing too much. The first game I played Pendleton in center and Ozark on first. In the second game I played Belardi on first and Pendleton in center. We won both games, as I recall, and were heading out of town to end up the season on the road.

After the game Mr. Rickey came into the clubhouse quite

pleased with everything, especially our showing in the double-header.

We had a meeting, going over some things, talking about the players, the veterans and the youngsters.

"Now you can't lose this thing," Mr. Rickey said to me, "so there's only one thing I want you to do the rest of the season. I want you to play Belardi on first and Pendleton in centerfield."

"Mr. Rickey," I said, "I wish we could go ahead and win the thing—clinch the pennant first. Then I'm willing to experiment with the young players as much as you want."

I made the mistake of adding a postscript. "I don't want to upset the players by doing this too soon and flirting with losing the lead. These guys have busted their butts all season to get this six-game lead. Experimenting with the kids now might affect the morale of the club."

That was an error.

"If you can't handle the morale of your ball club any better than that," he snapped back, "I don't want you to manage."

"OK," I replied, "if that's the way you want it, it suits me."

We went on to Kansas City. They, along with Indianapolis, were giving us trouble. Indianapolis had been right on our tail almost all year and were playing real good ball.

Against Kansas City, which was a big Yankee farm club then, we lost one, we lost two. Indianapolis won two. We lost three games in a row and Indianapolis won four. It kept going along like that to where we were down to a game and a half lead.

"I'm not going to call him," I said to myself. He made the rule and I was going to sink with it.

About 3 A.M. one morning the phone rang in my hotel room. It was Rickey. "Go ahead and use your own judgment from here on."

I thought to myself, isn't that great. We've got a game and a half lead with three or four to play. Actually what it came down to was a doubleheader on the final day of the season and we have to win them both to take the pennant by a half a game.

We won the doubleheader and the pennant, but in the play-offs Milwaukee, who had finished third, eliminated us in the first series, four games to three.

Just the same, those two years in St. Paul must have made a great impression on Mr. Rickey, and I feel today that those were the years that made me as a manager.

16

A SHORT TIME after the close of the season at St. Paul Mr. Rickey called me. He was moving me to Montreal as manager for the 1950 season, he said. Clay Hopper, who had been at Montreal, would switch to St. Paul.

There was no doubt that was a promotion. As far as Mr. Rickey was concerned, Montreal was Brooklyn's number one farm club. Most baseball men then would admit that the International League was the best of the Triple A minor leagues. To say I was pleased at the change would be an understatement.

I'd been managing for ten years—except for 1943 when I was strictly a player for Rochester—and Mr. Rickey must have felt I was ready for bigger and better things.

In the winnowing-down process that led to a job in Brooklyn there were many places for a player or a manager to slip. So far I had been pretty successful, though, and in Montreal I was rejoining Buzzie Bavasi, with whom I'd had such a great time at Nashua in the New England League. I knew there would be no problem with the front office. Buzzie was one of the fine people and ran an excellent operation. About the only thing that worried me at all was being in a city where French was the primary language. But I figured that one way or the other we would get by.

We learned right off in 1950 that going from Florida to Canada was like changing seasons. It was nice and warm in spring training in Florida but Montreal in early April was still likely to be having freezing weather. We had to have both winter clothes and lighter ones for when summer really arrived, normally in late June.

In the four seasons we spent in Montreal we never finished worse than second. Being the team's number one farm club, we had all the Dodgers of the future coming through, and a few of the fellows on the way down closed out their careers with me.

Dad decided to come up for a visit during one of our home stands that first year. Since he had never been out of the United States he figured this was a good time to visit a foreign country.

His buddy, Hap Davish, came with him. They spent a week or two going over the train schedules figuring out how to time the trip to get to Montreal just as the team would get back home from a road trip.

I guess the best part of their trip was in the planning, plus Dad's antics at the border. He'd warned Hap about having to go through customs and that he'd better not have anything illegal in his suitcase. They only had one little old case each, but Dad had warned Hap time and again to be sure he knew how to open his bag, that if he fumbled or bungled it customs was likely to go through everything.

Hap tried the lock a time or two to be sure he knew how to do it. Each time he tried he fumbled it worse, and by the time the inspector arrived he was really a nervous wreck. Fortunately, there was no problem, and they reached Montreal about an hour or so before game time. I'd told them to come out to the park in a cab.

I don't know if either one of them had ever been in a cab before but it was a pretty good distance to the park and they accumulated a fare of about $3.50, a pretty substantial amount in 1950. Instead of one of them paying the $3.50, each of them paid for it. The cabbie just went right along with it and got a hefty tip to boot. When they told me, I darn near fell off the chair in the clubhouse.

The Montreal park in those days was pretty much like Ebbets Field, right in the heart of town. There were stores all around it and it was a very active business district. Living within walking distance of the park, I usually ate breakfast in a little restaurant by the park. Everyone, of course, spoke French. The first full day Dad and Hap were in town we went there for breakfast.

I'd set it up with a cute little French waitress that I'd mumble something in my best French, but no matter what, she was to bring me ham and eggs. "Gimme the same thing," Dad said. She reeled off a string of French which Dad took to mean she didn't understand.

"Tell her what I want," he said.

"Nothing doing," I said, "you guys are on your own. You come up here to visit and you order your own meal."

Well, there was the doggonedest conversation in Ohio English and French you've ever heard. But finally the young French girl couldn't keep her act straight and burst out laughing.

One day they decided they'd better go do a little shopping so they'd have something to take home to their wives. We lived twenty-five blocks or so from the main shopping area of Montreal, and I could have driven them down in the car. But I told them the traffic was awfully bad in downtown Montreal and the streetcar was the way to go.

There was a trolley that ran down St. Catherine Street to the center of the city. It was right out of the Toonerville Trolley cartoon strip. It looked just like it and usually it was packed solid with people.

It wasn't too crowded going down, but on the way home I picked out one that I thought would be packed by the time we got back to the park. Hap had a couple of packages under his arm and Dad was pretty well loaded down too. When we got on the trolley it was full so we all had to stand. The longer we stood the farther we were shoved into the back of the car.

Just about the time the trolley reached DeLormier Street where we had to get off, I shoved my way forward. They were talking when I reached the door. I yelled, "Come on, let's go, come on," and got off.

By that time the trolley was going again. They waved and hollered and I just kind of threw my hands up in the air. They had to go to the next stop a block or so away and walk back.

Montreal was a great experience. Dodie was going to Wittenburg University in Springfield, Ohio, then so she and Lela didn't come up until after classes were out. In the meantime I lived in a rooming house. All I needed was a place to sleep. I spent the rest of the day at the park.

One of our players was Sandy Amoros, a little Cuban outfielder, who spent seven years later on with Brooklyn and Los

Angeles. Sandy, who spoke Spanish and almost no English, lived in the same rooming house. Our landlady spoke French and not much more English than Sandy. I spoke English and no French worth mentioning. So here were the three of us trying to talk in three languages. Our only hope for understanding was when the landlady's daughter was around. She spoke English fluently. They were nice people and we had a lot of laughs. Once in a while they'd have me in for breakfast and that was quite a treat.

Our second year in Montreal we won the pennant with a 95–59 record. We went into the playoffs and eliminated Buffalo in the first series in four straight. Then we beat Syracuse four games to one to represent the International League in the Junior World Series against Milwaukee. We finally lost to the American Association champions, Milwaukee, in a seven-game series.

Things were a little skittish in 1951. Right after the close of the 1950 season—October 26, in fact—Branch Rickey resigned as president of the Brooklyn Dodgers. Control of the club had been acquired by Walter F. O'Malley. Now, Walter had been with the club ever since Rickey, O'Malley and John Smith had acquired 75 percent of the club stock from the Ebbets and Ed McKeever heirs.

It was the first year, really, that I had not been working directly under Mr. Rickey but our season in 1951 with Montreal was superior. Little did I know then how many years I would be spending with Walter O'Malley, one of the finest men I've ever known and probably the greatest executive in baseball history.

In September of 1951 another event took place that has had a great influence on our lives. Our daughter, Dodie, had met a young fellow from North Manchester, Indiana, at Wittenburg in the spring of her freshman year and it was love almost at first sight.

Anyway, Harry Ogle was going into the service, so instead of waiting until November of 1951 they were married in September in Montreal. Harry was stationed in New York in the Air Force and came up to Montreal almost every weekend that summer.

Those four seasons in Montreal found almost every Dodger come by going one way or the other but the great majority were on their way to the big league. It's pretty difficult for me to place players in their proper year.

Some of them, like Tom Lasorda, who now is one of my coaches for the Dodgers, spent all four seasons with me. Jim Gilliam, who has been one of my coaches since retiring in 1966 after fourteen years with the Dodgers, spent a couple years with me at Montreal.

Jim was one of the most versatile players we had. Primarily a second baseman, Gilliam could more than hold his own at third or in the outfield. And there was a game or two late in his career at Los Angeles when he filled in at first. All that playing experience makes him a very valuable coach.

We won back-to-back pennants in 1951 and 1952 at Montreal. After going all the way to the Junior World Series final in 1951 we finished on top in 1952, beat Toronto in the first series of the playoffs, four games to three, but lost the finals to Rochester, four games to two.

In 1953 we were second, which matched our finish the first year in 1950. But this time we went on to eliminate Buffalo, four games to two, and Rochester in four straight. We met Kansas City in the Junior World Series, winning it four games to one.

Probably the biggest day of 1953 came in August. On August 26 our grandson Robin Dean Ogle was born in Montreal. Harry was in Korea with the Air Force and Dodie was living with us.

There's been a lot of talk ever since Rob has grown up that he was named after Robin Roberts and Dizzy Dean. Now I don't know about that. All I said when Dodie told me his name was: "He's got two outstanding ball players attached to his name right away, and if he's as good as either one of those guys he'll be all right."

Baseball was big in Montreal the four years I was there. The French loved it and television didn't give us much competition so we drew good crowds. On top of that, the club did well, being in the championship series every year and having some real talented and colorful players on the club.

I've always believed that baseball is still a game. You ought to enjoy it, get some fun out of playing, yet give it everything you have. As long as I could get that out of a player I was pretty easy to get along with.

I've always felt that condition was vital to success, and I expected my players to report to training camp ready to work. If someone showed up fat and sloppy, he had a lot to do before he'd get much of my time. My feeling is that if a man doesn't take enough pride in the game to take care of himself he won't go far in baseball.

At one time we had curfews and once or twice in my early years I went off on a wild goose chase to find a player who was violating the rules. But I've long since given that up.

One time I got an anonymous call that Jim Pendleton was in a night spot. I got in my car to check it out. Finally I found the place and went inside. I wandered around in this dark, gloomy bar straining my eyes to try and pick him out. Finally I asked the bartender if he had seen Pendleton. "That's Pendleton's girl friend over there," he told me. "You can ask her." She told me he had just left, but it was so dark it was pretty hard to tell who was anywhere.

I confronted him the next day and he tried to wiggle out of it. Finally he admitted he had slipped out one door as I came in another.

My theory is that you can have all the rules in the world but you can't really enforce them, especially in the big cities. If you try to play detective you'll spend more time checking up than teaching. I would rather try to convince the players to take care of themselves for their own good and let them be the policeman.

I never did run what you'd call a tight ship. Some of my coaches, like Tommy Lasorda, believe I'm not as loose and close to the players as I once was. No doubt part of that comes from being older and more experienced as a manager. And the mere fact that in Los Angeles we're spread out over half of Southern California rather than living within a few blocks of Dodger Stadium makes it hard to be close.

Back when Tommy was pitching for me at Montreal we were a tight little clique. It's pretty difficult to make new friends when you don't speak French fluently.

I had all kinds of gimmicks going then. I'd post a list of players I could beat playing pool, some I could beat in a foot race, others I could beat playing golf, and even a list of those I could beat in a game of hearts.

I remember one time playing hearts with Tom and the late Don Hoak, who was a fine infielder. My partner, as I recall, was Rocky Nelson, a first baseman with us. We weren't doing too well until suddenly it dawned on me that darn Lasorda and Hoak had put together a signal system.

Back in those days I pitched batting practice almost every day. In Syracuse, New York, there was a big clock out on the fence in right centerfield that we'd check out to see when our thirty minutes was up. It seemed like I was throwing forever, and when finally the bell rang I told Clyde King: "That's the longest thirty minutes I have ever thrown in my life."

"Walt," King said, laughing, "didn't you see Lasorda moving that clock back two or three minutes every time? You were out there about forty minutes."

I chased that gimpy-armed lefthander all over that outfield but he was too quick for me.

In Montreal we used to have a game every year among the team. The pitchers would play the regulars, and I always threw for the pitchers because we didn't want to waste an arm. It was a regular nine-inning game. When that was over, there wasn't much left in the old arm to pitch batting practice the next few days.

Ottawa, for some reason, always gave Montreal trouble, even when they were well down in the standings. One day we were in Ottawa and Lasorda was pitching. Mr. Rickey insisted each of his farm clubs work on and use the six-man infield. That's needed when there is a definite bunt in order. You bring the outfielder from the batter's side to first base to hold the runner close. With the runner on first, you bring the first baseman in tight on the grass along the first-base side. The third baseman is in close on the third-base side, and the pitcher charges straight in.

On this particular day Lasorda is pitching. It's the last of the eighth and we need a double play to get out of the inning. The batter bunts directly back to Tom, the perfect double-play ball, and he throws it clear into centerfield. That really riled me, and by the time we'd lost the game and I had reached the clubhouse, I grabbed the first chair I could find, put it up over my head, and slammed it down on the chow table, smashing everything in pieces.

I'm sure there were a lot more little things than I can remember that happened along the way in my years as a manager. For some reason more things stand out from Montreal.

We were still a train league in those years and every time we boarded a train we posted a list showing who was sleeping where. I've already mentioned that the regulars and the next day's starting pitcher were in lowers, and all the rest in uppers.

On one trip I was asleep and heard a knock at my compartment door. By the time I opened it I could see Chico Fernandez, a young shortstop from Havana, walking down the aisle toward his berth muttering in his broken English about having to sleep in an upper. He had been playing regularly but had been out of the lineup a few days with an injury. I chased him down the aisle and caught him.

"Look, buddy," I told him, "if you pop off to me one more time you'll be sleeping in the bathroom."

Years later Lasorda told me he had put Chico up to protesting, but there was no sign of Lasorda's head sticking out from the Pullman curtains that night.

Lasorda always was a needler and instigator of things but he was also a solid baseball man who knew the game and worked hard at being a good minor league pitcher. I'll never forget his complaint about not being called up to the Dodgers in 1955 after he'd won about twenty games two years in a row at Montreal.

We had room on the major league roster for only one more lefthander and Tommy wanted that spot. He had a meeting with Buzzie. They talked and talked but Tom wasn't gaining any ground.

"Who's going to be on the Dodger roster?" he finally asked Bavasi. "Why can't I be on it?"

All Buzzie finally said was: "Koufax."

Tommy knew he had lost the argument because any bonus player who was signed in those days had to spend two years on the major league club's roster. So there was no way we could send Sandy—who hadn't realized his greatness yet—down without losing him.

Lasorda was one of the hardest working players I've ever had. He eventually came up to Brooklyn two or three times but never could stay. He had trouble controlling his curve ball, and one time he bounced one over Campanella's head. Roy scrambled back to get it and Tommy raced in to cover the plate as the runner charged in to score.

There was quite a collision, but Tommy didn't show any

signs of being hurt as he went back to the mound to continue pitching. After the inning he walked past me to get his jacket. I could see blood covering his pants.

"What happened, Tommy?" I asked.

"Oh, nothing, skipper. Not a thing."

I grabbed him by the arm and demanded to see the leg. There was blood pouring out of a gash above his kneecap and the trainer hustled him into the clubhouse and out of the game. Tommy never lacked for courage nor color.

But those four years in Montreal were great ones. And there were a lot of great people, some of whom made it big in Brooklyn and some who never quite had that little something that makes a major leaguer out of a minor leaguer.

17

THE BROOKLYN DODGERS were in full flower in 1954. They'd been a dominant force in the National League for three successive years under Charlie Dressen.

In 1951 they ended up in a tie and lost the playoff to the Giants. They'd come back in 1952 to beat the Giants out by 4½ games with a 96–57 record. And in 1953 they put together one of the great records of all time winning by 13 games, with 105 wins and only 49 defeats. That meant they won 68.2 percent of their games—truly remarkable.

But neither year had they been able to beat the Yankees in the World Series. While the Dodgers were great, I guess you'd have to say that the Yankees were super as they won in 1952, four games to three, and in 1953, four games to two.

There was no doubt in my mind that I'd be back at Montreal

in 1954 despite all I'd read and heard about Charlie Dressen demanding a long-term contract from O'Malley. So, as in every other winter for almost twenty years, I was spending a great deal of my time hunting with Dad and our lifelong friend Howard Cox, the guy we'd set up with the hawk wired in the tree. We'd left Darrtown fairly early the morning of November 23—and I remember the date because it was one of the first days of hunting season. We'd driven around near Jericho looking for game and I'd done pretty well, coming home with a bird and three rabbits.

It had been a good day for Dad, Coxie and me. It was cold and crisp but nice hunting weather. The day was pretty well gone when we headed back to Darrtown, laughing and joking along.

When we pulled up in front of the house in Coxie's car, Lela came out. "Buzzie's been calling all day," she said. "He won't say what it's about but it's important. You're to call him right away."

All Buzzie told me was to get to New York right away. There was a plane ticket for me in the name of Matt Burns at the Cincinnati airport.

There wasn't much time for me to pack, get dressed and get to the airport. I didn't even ask Buzzie what was so important. I knew they wouldn't be calling me to come to New York for some routine meeting.

About a week before there had been a story in the *New York Mirror* that I had been offered the job as Dodgers' manager. "It can't be authentic," I told the Associated Press man who called. "I haven't heard anything about it."

That was true. "I haven't heard a word from Brooklyn since the season ended in Montreal," I insisted. "I haven't thought too much about the job and I'd have to talk to club officials."

Even in my brief conversation with Buzzie I didn't ask what he wanted. I did guess that if they were calling me in they at least wanted to talk to me about the job. I'd had two good years at St. Paul and four very good ones in Montreal. But in my own mind I couldn't believe that Charlie Dressen was going to push so far that he'd lose what I considered the best managing job in baseball.

As I packed and dressed and got to talking to Lela about going as "Matt Burns" (who was then a purchasing agent or something like that with Brooklyn) the more I began to speculate as to the purpose of the meeting. Lela's brother, Cliff Alexander, who passed away during the 1975 season, volunteered to drive me to the Cincinnati airport and we barely made the plane. All the way east I thought about the trip and the fact that I was going as Matt Burns. More and more it became apparent that Buzzie and Mr. O'Malley wanted more than just an interview with me.

As I was waiting for my luggage at La Guardia Field I heard a name being paged but I didn't pay any attention.

"Paging Mr. Matt Burns. Paging Mr. Matt Burns." Finally I realized that was me.

When I answered the page it was a man from the ball club who was to drive me directly to the Roosevelt Hotel.

"You don't have to register," the driver told me. "Just go up to this suite."

He handed me a piece of paper with a room number on it, and as we drove in from La Guardia to the hotel I became more and more certain I was going to be offered the job of managing the Dodgers.

I'm not real sure, but I think I carried my own bag up to the suite in the Roosevelt. When I knocked on the door, Buzzie let me in. Waiting with Buzzie were the late Fresco Thompson, who was a vice-president in charge of the farm system; Al Campanis, now the general manager of the Dodgers but then one of the chief scouts; and Bavasi.

"Walter, we'd like you to manage the Dodgers," Bavasi said, with no preliminaries. For the first time a long-standing dream was reality.

There was no doubt about my reaction. I wanted the job, and we spent a great part of the night talking over things. Somewhere along the line we finally got around to salary. My salary that year at Montreal was somewhere between $13,000 and $14,000.

"I want the job most of all," I told Buzzie, "and I'd like you to give me as much salary as you think you can."

"How about $24,000?" Buzzie asked. That was just fine with me. So on November 23—no, it was probably the next day by then—I was the Dodger manager at almost double my Montreal salary.

Once I'd agreed, I wanted to call Lela and my folks. That

was OK with Buzzie but they couldn't tell another soul until after a press conference he'd planned for the afternoon papers November 24.

Lela never got off the phone the next day. As soon as the Dodgers told the papers about the afternoon press conference, writers began trying to figure out who it was. Lela handled it well. She told everyone I was out hunting and wouldn't be back until late in the afternoon. One guy kind of flustered her, she told me later, when he asked: "You're sure he's not out hunting for the Dodger job in New York?"

Early that day I had slipped over to the old Brooklyn offices at 215 Montague Street. We had a long meeting with Mr. O'Malley, Buzzie, Fresco, Al and all the others present to prepare for the press conference that was called for the afternoon.

I'd never been in a formal press conference before and never one as big as this with as much at stake. Everyone from Walter O'Malley on down coached me a little on what to do and what not to do. They'd found me a Brooklyn uniform shirt and a cap with a scroll B on it to wear for pictures.

"You'll have to be careful what you say," Buzzie had warned me in the wee hours the night before. "They'll really probe." Now I'd talked to the press for years but hardly ever with any of the big shots from New York. And never before a television camera.

One of the rumor stories before I went to New York said: "Alston has a reputation for silence as pronounced as that of Chuck Dressen for loquacity."

That was in a story by Dan Daniels—the famous baseball writer of the *New York Times*. He also carried a quote from Mr. O'Malley in that same story, which perhaps was the indication of what was to happen. "Walter Alston is an estimable gentleman," O'Malley told Daniels, "or we would not have entrusted the Royals [Montreal] to his care."

There was a little pressure at the press conference. Some of the guys didn't know me at all. A few had met me in spring training over the years.

I put on the Dodgers' jersey and cap and the flash bulbs popped, the TV cameras rolled and so did the questions. They came from all sides and on all subjects, but most pertained to baseball and my life in the game and off the field.

94

When I woke up the next morning I was all over the sports page. I'll never forget the headline in the *New York Daily News:*

ALSTON (WHO'S HE)
TO MANAGE DODGERS

Maybe that stung a little bit. I don't really remember but I still have it in a scrapbook at home so it couldn't have bothered too much.

Most of those sportswriters over the years became fine friends and followed the Dodgers for many seasons. I'll always remember Frank Graham's column the next day in the *New York Journal-American.* He treated me kindly and so did the fellow who wrote the little headline for "Graham's Corner," as it was called:

Nobody knew Alston **24 hours ago**	**Now the world knows** **all about him**

FAME OVERNIGHT

One paragraph which probably didn't mean a lot to the readers or perhaps to Frank Graham did to me:

"If his first experience as the central figure in a high-powered publicity melee was wearing upon him, he gave no sign of it. He was composed, patient, responsive, dignified."

I spent a couple of days in Brooklyn going over things with Buzzie and the rest of the staff as we looked ahead to spring training of 1954 in Florida. It was a hectic time but one I'd waited a lifetime for.

Now at forty-two the opportunity was mine. Confidence I had but there was also a little concern.

Remember, this was Dressen's team. He'd put it together over the past three years and it had been very successful. But in going over the roster I found that I had managed twenty-five of the players at one point or another in their minor league career.

I was not a flamboyant, outgoing person like Dressen, but I knew what it took to put a team together and to win. I'd known a lot of the guys—fellows like Roy Campanella, Don New-combe, Duke Snider, Peewee Reese and Jim Gilliam—over the years. They came to play baseball and I was sure they'd play baseball for me.

Buzzie drove me to the airport so I could get home for Thanksgiving. And if ever a man had something to give thanks for it was me. It was still hard to believe. It only seemed like an hour ago that Dad, Coxie and I were out in the fields near Jericho hunting birds and rabbits.

Now as I flew back to Dayton and my family, I knew how I felt and I could just imagine how Dad felt. He was just bustin' his buttons because his boy was in the big leagues.

18

WHEN I REACHED the house at the corner of Cherry and Apple in Darrtown, all the family was there. There couldn't have been a happier bunch in the world, and we had quite a time. Unlike a lot of celebrations, however, there was not any booze. I'm almost a non-drinker. I say almost because when we win a championship I usually take one sip of the champagne. Liquor isn't for me. It doesn't agree with me and I never have liked it.

But the house was jumping nevertheless. Lela, Mom and Dad, Dodie and Harry and even little Rob, who was only about three months old, were there. A lot of the neighbors dropped by in the next day or two, and the house, which was just a little over a year old, sure filled the bill.

The house is something special for all of us, mainly because Mom and Dad laid up all the brick facing, built the fireplace and chimney, and supervised the whole thing.

We had been saving for years to build a house in Darrtown. Those Junior World Series checks—we had about $15,000—from Montreal and St. Paul gave us the extra cash we needed for a house. We had been looking around for some small acreage outside Darrtown to buy and build on, but after figuring closer, we found there wouldn't be too much left for construction when we paid for the land.

Dad owned the four acres directly across Apple Street and gave me two lots on the corner which were half acre lots. On the back of the very corner lot was the barn we had turned into a shop and stable. We finally made the decision to go ahead in the spring of 1952 just before I left for spring training with Montreal.

I doubt if another house has ever been staked out the way Dad and I did ours. It had been planted as a corn field, and there were still a lot of old dried stalks around after they had husked the corn. We picked up four corn stalks and staked out where we wanted the house to be, facing Cherry. Dad's house faced on Apple.

There were these four corn stalks sticking up like four old skinny scarecrows and that was all Dad had to go on to build a house. I made an agreement with Glenn Ward, a building contractor in Darrtown, to handle everything, with the provision that he would dig the foundation but Dad would do all the brick work, the brick veneer.

Dad mixed all his own mortar. He was a meticulous brick layer. Everything had to be level and straight. If a pebble was out of plumb Dad would correct it.

Mom was out there every day helping. Dad did all the heavy work but Mom handed him every brick. There's a pattern to the bricks—one red and one tan—and Mom made sure that Dad got the right one as he laid them up. They are all straight as a string but I think his nicest work was the stonework on the front of the house. Laying up the stonework was really difficult and you appreciate how well Dad did the job if you look down the line and see how perfect they are set.

You know, I really didn't have much more to do with that house than staking out the corn stalks. By the time I got back from Montreal in October or so the house was all done.

We've made an addition or two over the years. Harry and

97

Dodie eventually decided to move in since we were gone almost nine months of the year. After Kimberly Kay came in 1957 as our first granddaughter and Lela's mother moved in, we made a large addition.

We created our recreation room where my pool table and trophies take up most of the space, and we built on a large bedroom and bath for Dodie, so now we have a five-bedroom ranch-style house.

Once again Dad did all the necessary brick and stonework. He made almost a perfect match. He even did the stonework around the mailbox out in front of the house.

We have a large nearly full basement downstairs and every one in the family has a little specialty area. I've got a darkroom where I can process my own film. There is also an area where I can reload my shotgun shells. We built a huge train table for Robbie, and there is also a table tennis rig. Harry and Dodie designed the track for the train and put it all down.

We have freezers down there, laundry facilities, and ironing equipment. That's also where Dodie strips down antiques and refinishes them. The basement is probably the biggest room in the house, but it serves a lot of purposes.

It is really remarkable that four generations live under one roof and there are never any wars. It's one big happy family. Everyone does his own thing, yet we do a lot of things together. No one has a quick temper, we're all pretty low key, and we have a lot of common likes.

Of course, we do create a lot of confusion among first-time visitors with our names. Everyone has at least two. It all began when Robin fell in love with Roy Rogers on TV. He named his grandmother Dale so now she answers to Lela or Dale. He named me Pat, after Roy's helper, and you can imagine who was Roy—Rob. He called his pony Trigger and a dog he had at the time was Bullet. Now Doris is our daughter's given name but she is Dodie, too. Most people call Kimberly Kim or Kimmie, but somewhere along the line I started calling her Sam so she will answer to any of the three.

Rob's father, Harry, didn't get into the Rogers act so I began to call him Jack. Once in a while he'll retaliate and call me Jackson.

Rob never had the nerve to name his mother or his Grandma Grace Alexander. My dad added a bit to the confusion for a long time by calling Lela Joe every now and then. We never did figure out how he came up with Joe but every once in a while one of us will call her Joe and she will answer.

Most of my friends around Darrtown call me Smokey, but seldom Walter. But hardly anyone in the family ever uses Smokey.

Someone coming into the house for the first time could go crazy trying to figure out who was who.

After my mother died Dad came over every night for dinner. That made eight of us and there was a lot of kidding. We always had a little pool game after dinner but now it's only Harry and I. Robbie plays when he's around but that's only at Christmas time.

Everything is kind of a joint effort around the house. Meals are a family project, and with more than four acres of grass to mow, everyone chips in and takes his turn on the power mower. Only thing is, I don't get too much time since we're gone in summer and the truth of the matter is that Dodie runs the mower most of the time.

Dodie's a pretty good outdoor girl. I remember when she was little and got Dad to build her a birdhouse. She kept warning him not to make the hole too big. She wanted it so only wrens could get in, not sparrows. When it was all done, Dad gave Dodie the brace and bit that would make it just right for a wren.

"This is a brand new bit," he warned her, "and I don't know if you are familiar with a brace and bit but there is a ratchet on it and it'll only turn and cut one way."

He showed her how it worked on another piece of wood but just before he gave it to her he flipped the ratchet so it would reverse and not cut a lick. She was grinding and grinding and grinding away and no hole. He had warned her how sharp it was and how quick it cut and to be careful she didn't rip through the wood.

Standing behind the door watching her grind away, Dad finally let his laughter get the best of him. Then Dodie knew she had been taken in by another of his pranks. She called him a few names but it was all in fun.

I guess it's things like this that have kept all of the family congenial and happy.

We've played bridge every night during the winter for years.

It's a perpetual contest. Maybe we'll start out with Harry and me as partners against Lela and Dodie. We play to 10,000 points per match and start over. You have to win two out of three matches. Last year, we got three rounds in, so you can see we play a lot of bridge. We usually break to watch the eleven o'clock news. Once we have won two out of three we'll switch partners and start over.

I've played cards as long as I can remember. I guess my grandmother got me started as a kid, but we didn't start to play bridge until we built our house and I became manager of the Dodgers. In the minor leagues there weren't many bridge players.

Over the years, however, there have been quite a few with the Dodgers. I guess we really got started on a more or less regular basis when Doc Wendler was the Dodger trainer and we played with our wives quite a bit. During the years when Don Drysdale, Jim Gilliam and Wes Parker were playing for us we played a lot of bridge on the road. But in recent years we just haven't had four bridge nuts on the club.

It's a great game. Keeps your mind active. It really requires concentration and takes you away from baseball for a little while.

We played most of our bridge in spring training at Vero Beach. Since the players couldn't come back in the press room we usually played out in the lobby. Sometimes we'd have quite a few kibitzers around.

We've even had a little expert help a time or two. Charles Goren, who is among the top bridge players of all time, once played a few hands in the clubhouse while we were still in Brooklyn. I don't remember who the fourth was but Goren, Pee Wee Reese and I were three of the foursome.

Not too many years back Goren came to Vero and was my partner against Wes Parker and Jim Gilliam. I must have been pretty much of a liability for Goren because Parker, who is pretty good and holds some master points, and Gilliam beat us.

They felt pretty good because Goren has a little card he gives to people he plays if they should win. It's the size of a calling card and says "I beat Goren."

We played a lot of bridge that winter following my selection as Dodger manager but there wasn't any game for a night or two. Everything had come so suddenly we spent a lot of time talking about my new job and what a great opportunity it was. And of course at one time or another everyone we knew in Darrtown and the surrounding area came by.

One thing for sure, the time between being hired and the day to depart for Florida really flew by. Before I knew it, it was time to pack and head south. But this was different from all the years before. Now I knew who would be on my club and could spend my energy being the man in charge of the Brooklyn Dodgers on the field.

19

I WASN'T WORRIED about the mechanics of managing in the major leagues. There really isn't a great deal of difference between handling a club in a Triple A league like St. Paul or Montreal and handling the Dodgers in the National League. I was confident of my ability and confident that I could relate to the players.

But there was concern. I was coming in behind Charlie Dressen, my total opposite in personality, mannerism, and relations with the press. There was only one way for me to play it and that was my way. I'd be different, no question, but I hoped that the difference would end up with the same result—a pennant.

Dressen and the Dodgers had won back-to-back National League pennants in 1952 and 1953 but couldn't get that World Championship flag that all of Brooklyn wanted so desperately. You must remember that Brooklyn had never won a World

Series, and this rankled Walter O'Malley more than a bit, I am sure.

As we drove from Ohio to Florida there were many hours wheeling south down the highway to think about the months ahead and our 152-game schedule.

The fact that the Dodgers were made up of experienced players, men who had achieved a great deal, knew their jobs well and were intimately aware of what it took to win could be a plus or a minus for a rookie manager. I considered it only one way. A plus. I knew them all and knew what they could do. When you have names like Roy Campanella, Gil Hodges, Jackie Robinson, Pee Wee Reese, Billy Cox, Duke Snider, Carl Furillo, Don Newcombe, Clem Labine, Joe Black and the likes that spells talent.

It might also mean that Mr. O'Malley was expecting to see one of those World Series flags flying on the flagpole in Ebbets Field at the end of the 1954 season. But as we cruised toward Vero Beach, I remembered the press conference in the Dodger office when I was announced as the manager.

One of the writers asked O'Malley about whether I would be faced with winning a World Series or else in that first year.

"There is no one more dedicated to winning a World Series than I am," Mr. O'Malley explained. "And we think Walter Alston is the man who can do it."

He turned toward me as I sat there with my suit coat off, wearing a home Dodger shirt. "Walter," he said, "we're not going to be breathing down your neck. You don't have to win the pennant.

"If you have to be fired," and as I recall he had that infectious twinkle in his eye, "it wouldn't be because you failed to win. We've never fired a manager for failure to win unless the failure was his own doing." There was a hearty laugh from among the writers but I thought I understood what the boss meant. That if I did my best and for some reason that was beyond my control we stumbled I would be back.

"I'd like to think," I remember him adding, "you'll be the manager for a great many years."

While at the time I didn't know Walter O'Malley very well, I did feel he was a sincere, honest man and I approved of the team concept of running a major league organization.

I wasn't concerned about having only a one-year contract.

That's what I had had every year since I'd joined the Dodger system with Branch Rickey back at Trenton in 1944.

Later on during that first press conference, O'Malley was asked about his insistence on giving his managers only a one-year contract. It was a demand by Charlie Dressen for a long-term contract that had resulted in his dismissal.

"If a man does the job we expect of him," O'Malley explained, "he can expect to be back the next year. He doesn't need a long-term contract as his job guarantee."

Little did I realize then how many of those one-year-at-a-time contracts I was going to sign both in Brooklyn and Los Angeles.

I could hardly wait to reach Vero Beach and those old Navy Air Corps barracks that the Dodgers had converted into our living quarters. They weren't what you would call plush, more like strictly G.I. But a lot of players went through that compound over the years and any of them who were among the group can recite stories that never end.

The walls were paper thin and if the weather turned cold you needed a lot of blankets to keep warm. If too many electric heaters were tied in, fuses kept blowing and creating all kinds of problems. When we look back on them now from our present commodious quarters, it brings back a lot of memories.

As Lela and I drove into the grounds that February it was one of the biggest days of my life. And when I pulled on that Dodger uniform for the first time with number 24 on its back a dream of years was finally realized.

I was a fortunate guy. Not only was I taking over a fine, experienced ball club that first year but I had a coaching staff loaded with major league experience. Billy Herman, who had played second base for Brooklyn and the Cubs and managed the Pirates and Red Sox, was one of my coaches. So was Jake Pitler, one of the many career men in the Dodger system whom I'd known for years. Ted Lyons, a legend for twenty-one years as a pitcher for the White Sox and their manager for three years, was my pitching coach.

Back in those days many managers were active on the field and I was among them that first year. I coached at third base. It was Buzzie Bavasi who insisted that I do that. As I look back on it, I think he wanted me out there every day so everyone would recognize me. While I had managed for many years my time in the major leagues was literally nil, whereas most of my coaches had been around for years and were all well known. I agreed that working the third base coaching box was the thing to do.

But after a year I went to the bench and I haven't been out on the field since. I feel a manager is better off on the bench than in the box. He can talk to hitters before they go up to the plate. He can also talk to the players about other things because the prime point of concentration is not the base runner or the batter but an overview of the whole situation.

Over the years many people have asked me if it has been a handicap managing in the big leagues when I didn't really play. I don't think so. There have been many managers who have had outstanding records with very meager major league careers. Some like Joe McCarthy never got to the big leagues. I do think it would be an advantage for a player—say like Brooks Robinson, who has played so brilliantly so many years for Baltimore—to take over a team immediately after quitting as a player. Then he would have intimate knowledge of the teams he had to beat. But otherwise I don't think so.

I was definitely on the spot when I took over the Dodgers, and it began with the first day at Vero Beach. A veteran club, the Dodgers had won the pennant two years in a row. Every writer and every expert picked us to repeat. That was a tough assignment, not because I was a new manager but because I just didn't think the club could possibly have a year like 1953.

How could you win 105 games again? How could you beat the Giants by 13 games again? How could you win 68 percent of your games?

I was skeptical because literally every man had a great year in '53. I felt it was expecting a lot for all of them to repeat with great years. That seldom happens.

It didn't worry me. I went to work in Vero Beach to do the best job I knew how. I wanted each man to have the best year he could have. I've never let the job worry me. You can't ever replay yesterday's game; all you can do is prepare for tomorrow's.

A great many things were going for me my first year. We were solid at almost every position. I had three strong, dependable leaders in Reese, Hodges and Campanella. They could have made it awfully tough if they wanted, but they were with me and made it easy instead. They worked right with me as did every other man on the roster.

Now there has been a lot of talk over the years about the problems I had with Jackie Robinson. First off, that's wrong. I had no more problems with Robinson than some others, but what there were were magnified by his stature. Robinson in his day was a great baseball player, perhaps one of the greatest all-around athletes there has ever been.

There's no doubt when I took over in 1954 that it wasn't the same Jackie Robinson who led the blacks into baseball in 1946 when he was signed by Mr. Rickey. He was still a fine, fine baseball player—one who was terribly intimidating in almost any situation. But he had been with the Dodgers seven years. He was thirty-five years old and had lost some of his speed but none of his skills.

Those who claimed there was a feud between us were dead wrong. We only had a misunderstanding. I think Jackie wanted to test the rookie manager. He did and he got the answer.

By that time Robinson was in his eighth season with Brooklyn. He had starred on four championship teams and had been in four World Series. He had played second, third, first and in the outfield. He was a consistent .300 hitter who could go with the wind and, until Maury Wills came along, was probably the most intimidating base runner of his day.

He was an inspiring player, a born leader who could literally lift a team. But most important he had faced and survived probably the greatest challenge any major league player ever did— he broke the color barrier and won.

If ever a man came to play the game of baseball Jackie Robinson did. We had our differences early on, perhaps the third or fourth day of spring training. I had noticed that Robinson wasn't a very enthusiastic participant in the calisthenics that opened our practice each day. He was often late. Or he was off chatting to someone. Usually a writer.

I talked to him privately about it one day. He didn't like it, I know, but he did make the field on time and take part in the exercises after that. Then during one of our early exhibitions I rested Jackie to get a long look at some of the young fellows. He was supposed to be on the bench in case he was needed.

The next thing I realized, he was out in the bullpen chatting with a writer. That violated two rules. The writer didn't belong out there. Jackie shouldn't have been talking with him. The place for them to talk was the clubhouse after the game.

The next day I called a clubhouse meeting. Explained the rules about being on the bench and about talking to writers. They weren't new. They'd been the Dodgers' rules for years. Jackie had a habit of talking to others during clubhouse meetings and when I made my points about the bench and writers he talked back a little.

Our conversation got a little rough. I called him on it and told him and everyone else that they could talk to me any time, any place and about anything. Now some of the players felt that was a physical challenge by me of Jackie. Possibly it could have been interpreted that way.

I do know that there was an inference that if Robinson wanted to test me man-to-man that was OK with me. Roy Campanella, one of my all-time favorite people, helped calm the storm. Jackie and I were never near blows.

I felt this about Robinson then and still do: The longer we were together—and it was only three years before he retired rather than go to the Giants in a trade—the better our relations. They were better the second year than the first and the third year than the second.

There was never any question about Jackie Robinson's ability as a player, nor any question of his status as a man. I think that deep down that first year he felt the resentment toward a rookie manager that any outstanding player might feel, but that day in the clubhouse helped clear the air.

And the effort he put forth those three years was everything he had despite bad legs. You could still see the greatness in him as a player. Sometimes something he would do would be phenomenal. He, like Campy, Gil and Pee Wee, was best when you needed the best he had in him. You can't ask any more than that from anyone.

You know, I feel rather fortunate to have been in at the beginning of the blacks' introduction to organized baseball. Robinson got the credit for breaking the barrier and his conduct under the most trying circumstances was excellent. But in that same season—1946—I had had Campy and Newcombe at

Nashua and those two gentlemen made their mark in eliminating the racial barriers.

There's never been a time in my years since with the Dodger organization where I've felt we had a problem. We've always been a close club with a genuine feeling of togetherness among all the players no matter what their background. I know a lot of fine men have been with me over the years, starting with Campy and Newk, right down to today. You couldn't ask for better people or more superior players than two like Campy and Newk or Jim Gilliam, or John Roseboro, or Maury Wills or Davey Lopes or Al Downing or any of the others over the years.

That first year with Brooklyn was a wonderful year in all ways but one. We didn't win. Newcombe was back after two years in service, but he didn't look good in spring training and never really got in the groove he showed in 1951 when he won 20 and lost 9. He struggled all year. He started 29 games but completed only 6.

It wasn't his fault. He gave it everything he had but two years away from the competition of major league baseball was asking too much, even of a pitcher like Newk.

His loss was our biggest, but still we were neck and neck with the Giants most of the year only to lose out to them in the stretch. When we finished second, five games back, there were quite a few who pointed the finger at the rookie manager. But that's part of the game and I accepted it.

The one fear I had going into my first season as manager of Brooklyn was whether I could survive in the big city. For a farm boy it was strange to live in a high rise apartment at 1809 Albermarle Road in Brooklyn. I'd always scuffed the dirt off my shoes on the stoop and walked in the kitchen door. Now I had to push a button and ride an elevator.

We lived in the same apartment house with Billy Herman that year and that was good. Billy's wife and Lela spent a lot of time together and Billy taught me how to hop the subway and ride two stops on to Ebbets Field.

I can never say that I enjoyed being a city man, but I've spent more time in a big city the past twenty-two years than I have in the country. Yet any way you cut it I'm still a country guy at heart.

We took our car to Brooklyn that first year and that was a mistake. It cost us $75 a month to keep it in a garage and I don't think we took it out a dozen times. In fact, when it came time for us to drive back to Darrtown the battery was shot. We had to buy a new one before we could get the car out of the garage and on the road to Ohio.

20

THOSE MONTHS between the close of my first year as manager of the Brooklyn Dodgers and the opening of spring training at Vero Beach in 1955 flew by. Winters had always been pretty peaceful for me but I discovered being a big league manager also carried some demands I hadn't had to meet before.

I had a lot of requests to speak around Ohio. I'm not the most eloquent speaker now and I sure wasn't then. But speak I did. I also had to attend my first major league winter meeting. I didn't know whether I was going to enjoy sitting around a hotel for a week in meetings, but I've got to the point where I kind of look forward to them. It's about the only time you can sit down and just shoot the breeze with the other managers without worrying about the next pitch or who's coming up next. You get to know the men as men rather than as rival managers.

But I was eager to get back to Vero Beach for spring training despite some of the grumblings and criticism I had read in the winter. A rookie manager is always subject to second-guessing, and when we didn't win in 1954 there was probably more than usual. But I learned long ago that all I could do was my best and hope the players could do their best and between the two put together a winner.

Now some of the veteran writers who covered the Dodgers

and were critical of my performance in 1954 carried that attitude over into spring training. This was in a time when a club's readiness for the season was measured by the number of pitchers going nine innings.

As I recall, the only pitcher who had gone nine for us in Florida was Carl Erskine, and that was considered rather reckless. But I was convinced our starters were ready and so was our new pitching coach, Joe Becker. We also had some pretty good bullpen specialists, like Clem Labine and Don Bessent, who came up in midseason.

There was a little bit of fuel added on during the spring since we didn't have too good a won and lost record. I wasn't the least concerned. I felt we were in good shape. Don Newcombe, who struggled so long in 1954, was back to the Newcombe I'd remember before his two-year tour of service when he had a league-leading 164 strikeouts.

I didn't hear any objections from Buzzie Bavasi or Mr. O'Malley, and all my coaches felt our progress was right on schedule for the season opener.

A day or two before we opened the season, one newspaper carried a story saying that I made it one year as Dodger manager and now I would probably make it a second year, but there was trouble ahead.

I've never been one to be concerned about what I read or hear. I went to Vero that spring with no contract. One day Buzzie reminded me that we hadn't signed a contract, so after the workout we sat down and put one together. I got a little raise, as I recall, but I was never one to push for a contract. I just let them come along one year at a time. But the way some of the writers felt I might have signed my last in 1955.

Joe Becker, who was in his first year in the Dodger organization, had replaced Ted Lyons as pitching coach. He had caught a couple of years with Cleveland in the mid-thirties. We had managed against one another in the Western League when I was at Pueblo and he was at Sioux City. Then Buzzie knew Joe and we decided he'd be a good coach.

We'll never know if it was coincidence or what but we started off the 1955 season in unreal fashion. We set a National League record, as I recall, by winning our first ten games. The first six were won by six different pitchers, which was remarkable. Carl Erskine, Don Newcombe, Billy Loes, Russ Meyer, Johnny Podres and Clem Labine recorded those victories.

The streak was snapped when Marv Grissom, who later became quite a pitching coach, beat Podres for the New York Giants, 5–4. Then we started off another string, winning eleven more before losing.

It was probably one of the hottest starts in baseball history. We won 25 out of our first 29 games and had a 9½-game lead. We were the talk of baseball and Brooklyn was beside itself talking World Series and championship. And we hadn't even run into warm weather.

One thing that streak did was silence all my critics. I never really objected to criticism and I still don't. But I've always felt every fellow should have a chance. We lost four in a row early on and finally settled down into a solid groove. We seemed to be on a steady incline with very few valleys and no giant peaks.

By July 4 we were 12½ games in front and winging. We clinched the pennant in 1955 on September 8—then the earliest on record in the National League.

Even that created a little controversy. There was a lot of wondering going on if perhaps we hadn't clinched things too soon. Would we lose our edge? Would it have been better to have won it by four or five with a week or so to play?

Now baseball folk can argue that point forever. I didn't know the answer in 1955 and I don't know it now. I think there's a certain advantage to clinching the title with four or five days to go so you can rotate your pitchers around the way you want and get things set for the Series. I also think there is an advantage in playing in a tight pennant race, finally winning it with only a game or two to go and coming in with momentum on your side.

Which is the most important?

Over the years I've had a little of each, but I don't think there is any real edge to having to wait around a long while. And when you win by 13½ games as we finally did that might allow a bit of complacency to settle in.

It was rather ironic that Brooklyn hadn't been picked to win the pennant in 1955. The *Sporting News* poll in preseason favored Milwaukee, with the Giants and Dodgers figured to fight things out for second. They had the three clubs right, but the

110

order was reversed as we won, with the Braves second by 13½ and the Giants back in third by 18½.

It was a historic season in Brooklyn, and pretty hysterical, as we went into the World Series against Casey Stengel and the New York Yankees.

For me it was unforgettable. I'd seen only one Series and that was the year before when the Giants swept Cleveland in four. Now it was mine to win or lose. Literally everything ceased in the borough of Brooklyn. I don't think I've ever seen more baseball mania.

Brooklyn—the city, that is—was convinced this was the Dodger year. Winning so early and by such a large margin had convinced the fans of that. True, we were a solid ball club and things had gone our way almost all year. But New York was solid as well, and Stengel and the Yankees had been winning World Series a long while.

A lot of Brooklyn came tumbling down and I was right along with them when we lost our first two games in Yankee Stadium. Newcombe was bombed out in the sixth inning as we lost, 6–5. Then the Yanks jumped on Billy Loes early, getting four runs in the fourth on their way to a 4–2 triumph.

It was Stengel's sixth Series in seven seasons at New York. History and a lot of baseball experts were against our coming back to win. No club had ever come back to win the Series after losing the first two.

Brooklyn had been in eight World Series. The previous seven had all been failures. It was my first, and as we moved back to Ebbets Field for three games we were determined to beat history and win.

Johnny Podres was our selection to start the third game. The call fell on his twenty-third birthday. John gave us all a reason to celebrate, going the distance, allowing the Yanks only seven hits and winning, 8–3. The skeptics still pointed out that no club had ever come back from losing the first two games in all the years since the Series began back in 1903.

We evened things up the next day even though Carl Erskine, our sore-armed starter, was driven out in the fourth. The actual victory went to young Clem Labine, who went the final four and one-third innings. A truly strange incident occurred in this game. Don Larsen, the Yankee right-hander, ripped a pretty good foul ball back into the stands in the lower box seats. It bounced off the head of Del Webb, then a co-owner of the Yankees.

Things were all starting anew on Sunday, but we couldn't afford to lose and go back to Yankee Stadium down a game with two to play. There was a lot of public debate over our pitching selection, but within the club there wasn't.

We went with a rookie, Roger Craig, who had joined the club along about the middle of the season from Montreal. Roger had done real well for us, appearing in 21 games and starting 10. His 5 and 3 record wasn't overly impressive but his earned run average of 2.78 was excellent.

Our lineup was pretty well set for the Series. Roy Campanella did the catching, Gil Hodges was on first, Pee Wee Reese at short, Jackie Robinson at third, Duke Snider in centerfield and Carl Furillo in right. I platooned second base and left field. Jim Gilliam, who was an adept switch hitter, played second against right-handed pitchers and left field against left-handers. When Gilliam was in left, Don Zimmer was at second base. When Gilliam was at second, Sandy Amoros was in left.

Sandy gave Craig a big lift with a two-run home run off Bob Grim in the second inning. Roger did exceptionally well for a young guy in his first Series, going six innings officially before giving way to Labine. Labine, by the way, came out of the bull pen four times in the series to establish himself as a fine relief pitcher.

That 5–3 win gave us all a big lift.

For game six at Yankee Stadium, a lot of people expected that I might go with Don Newcombe. Even though he had lost the opener, he had been our big gun all year. But I decided to go with Karl Spooner, who might have a better chance in a park that favors left-handed pitchers.

The only problem was that another left-hander named Whitey Ford had one of his great days, throwing a four hitter and bringing everything down to game seven by beating us, 5–1. Later on I learned that this was the first time in history that a club started six different pitchers in the first six games of the Series.

Now we were down to one. There was no tomorrow, only today. Brooklyn needed a win for its first pennant. A Yankee victory would add another to their string and Casey's.

There was no doubt who I was going with. Podres. Johnny loved pressure. Really thrived on it. To me he was at his best with the most at stake. And on this Tuesday in New York he was in the cooker down there in the fire. But he wasn't alone. Every man on each club faced the same challenge.

Podres had completed only five games in twenty-four starts in the regular season but two of the five were shutouts. Ironically, none of his complete games came after June 12, which left some room for conjecture when he got my call to start game seven. But in tight spots Johnny was tough and now was as tight as they come.

Casey gambled in the fourth inning after Campanella doubled off starter Tommy Byrne. Hodges was up and Casey decided to pitch to him rather than walk him to get at Don Hoak. The young third baseman was playing for Jackie Robinson, who was pretty tired and a bit torn by the seventh game. His big problem was a bad foot.

Hodges worked Byrne around to where he singled to score Campy to give us a 1–0 lead.

Now one run isn't much against the Yanks, and in the sixth we added another with a hand from Lady Luck. Pee Wee Reese singled to bring up Duke Snider. He was bunting for a sacrifice, but when he brushed past first baseman Bill Skowron's glove tag trying to reach the bag, Duke knocked the ball away and we had runners on first and second.

Campy moved both of them along with a sacrifice. Stengel elected to walk Carl Furillo intentionally to fill the bases but it also brought Hodges up. Stengel decided to remove Byrne and replace him with Bob Grim. Then Hodges lifted a deep fly to left center that scored Reese and gave Gil his second run batted in for the day.

Up 2–0 now, I still wasn't comfortable against the Yankees with that lead. When Grim made a wild pitch to Hoak, Yogi Berra blocked the ball but couldn't find it rolling around near his feet. Furillo took second while Yogi was scrambling around. Then Grim walked Hoak.

Don Zimmer, who was playing second, was up next. I decided to go for a long ball and sent George (Shotgun) Shuba, who hadn't been in the Series before, to bat for him.

While my immediate strategy failed, batting Shuba for Zimmer required me to make an adjustment in the field. I brought Gilliam in from left field to replace Zimmer at second base and sent Sandy Amoros into left.

Billy Martin started the Yankees off in their half of the sixth with a walk. Gil McDougald beat out a surprise bunt single. With runners on first and second Berra came to the plate. In such a situation Yogi was even more dangerous than normal. He thrived on competition but he was up there against Podres, who was equal to almost any challenge.

Berra tied into one of John's high pitches and sliced a sinking fly ball into the right field corner. Sandy, playing a little bit toward left center for Berra, had a long, long way to come. I really couldn't see the ball too well from our dugout. All I knew when the stadium roar went up was that it was either a hit or a catch.

I could see our players set up for a throw so I knew it was caught. Both Martin and McDougald had taken off, figuring there was no way Amoros would catch the ball. Martin managed to scramble back to second in time, but Sandy's throw to Reese and the relay to Hodges was one of the finest double plays on McDougald I ever saw. Hank Bauer then grounded out to end the inning and for all intents and purposes the Series.

Now there was good fortune in my having had Shuba hit for Zimmer. If Gilliam had still been in left, from what the guys told me, it would probably have been impossible for Jim to get it. Since Gilliam is right-handed, his glove would have been on his left hand. Amoros, a left-hander, had his glove on his right hand and had just the few inches edge to make the catch.

I remember looking at the clock when Podres retired the final batter. It was 3:44 P.M. At that moment every place in Brooklyn must have come apart. Thirty years of waiting was over with John's 2–0 shutout.

It was the Dodgers' first World Championship. It was my first World Series win. It stopped a Yankee streak of seven world championships without a defeat and it ended Casey Stengel's string of never having managed a losing team in a World Series.

It was really Johnny Podres's hour. He'd won a big one for

us on Sunday, to take us back to Yankee Stadium. Now with three days' rest he had come back to shackle some of the great bats in baseball and win the big one. Twice I had gone out to the mound to talk with him but neither time was I close to taking him out. I had Clem Labine up ready to go in the eighth inning, but when John got Berra I decided to leave him in.

There was great joy in our clubhouse. A lot of champagne and beer was spilled. Far more went on the floor than down the throats of our screaming guys.

From Walter O'Malley on down, everyone in the Dodgers organization was thrilled beyond comprehension. It was a great win. A great hour for a bunch of guys who had an unbelievable year.

The celebration was really big in Brooklyn, as we found out when we tried to get home that night after the game. I'm sure no one went to bed until the wee hours.

And back in Darrtown Dad created a little celebration of his own. He told me he never left the TV set throughout the Series, but as soon as Elston Howard grounded to Pee Wee Reese and the ball hit Hodges's glove for the last out he let out a war whoop and ran out of the house.

He jumped into his pickup truck and drove down Main Street blowing the horn. A lot of the folks raised the American flag in their yards and before the sun had set someone had painted a WELCOME HOME SMOKEY sign in anticipation of our return.

My friend Earl F. (Red) Huber, who ran Darrtown's only tavern at the time, The Hitching Post, did a roaring business. Friends and folks came in from Oxford and Hamilton and when I got back they threw a big party at the Knights of Pythias Hall for the hometown boy who'd made it big as a major league manager.

I'd been interviewed and reinterviewed at the Stadium, in Brooklyn the next day and literally every second before I had a chance to sit down at home and read what all the writers said.

There weren't many knocks about Walter Alston and quite a lot of praise. It was great, especially for Brooklyn. Five times —1941, 1947, 1949, 1952 and 1953—they'd made the World Series only to lose. Now we'd won and we'd won against one of the best.

Of all the comments I recall from that first win in the World Series one stands out, and for the life of me I can't tell you who wrote it. Whoever it was compared Brooklyn's reaction to that win to the warning cry of one of the citizens of Hades who was exhorting the townspeople to flee.

"Get out. The Dodgers just won the World Series. All hell is freezing over."

Wonderful news. And it was going to make for an even more wonderful winter.

21

THAT WINTER of 1955 following our World Series success I don't think our phone ever quit ringing or the mailman ever passed our box without stopping.

I heard from old friends and older baseball acquaintances I hadn't heard from in years. I had numerous requests to speak at breakfasts, lunches and dinners. Finally I realized that I'd have to be selective or I was in trouble.

It's not that I wasn't pleased to have so many fine people wanting to talk with me or have me talk to them. But this was my first introduction to being in heavy public demand, and even though it was an honor, you just don't change a man's way of living overnight. It didn't seem fair to have to sacrifice so much of my vacation or to have so little opportunity to enjoy the quiet life of Darrtown.

Those weeks between the close of the Series in 1955 and the opening of spring training in late February in Vero Beach flew by. I remarked to my wife as we were packing that it just seemed like last week we were unpacking.

I didn't really find things much different in spring training in

1956 than in 1954 or 1955. Sure, we had a little more press around because we were champions. I had to spend a lot more time talking with them and there was greater demand for interview time with players, but that's the price of winning, and there isn't one of us in baseball who won't gladly pay that price.

We hadn't stood pat during the winter. Buzzie and Mr. O'Malley had made some trades, but basically we were going with the solid nucleus who had won for us in 1955. We'd acquired Ransom Jackson from the Cubs to try and fill third base where Jackie Robinson was running out of time. To get Jackson, however, we had to give up Don Hoak, a fine prospect who went on in later years to star with Cincinnati, Pittsburgh and Philadelphia.

We traded off pitchers Russ Meyer and Billy Loes to Chicago and Baltimore. We brought up two infielders—Charley Neal and Chico Fernandez—and outfielder Gino Cimoli from our farm system.

Still, our batting order was pretty much the same as in 1955. Campy, who had trouble with both hands all year, did most of the catching. Hodges was a fixture at first. Gilliam divided second base with Charley Neal, and when he wasn't there he was out in left field platooning with Sandy Amoros. Reese, even though he was now thirty-seven, was a solid shortstop.

Robinson and Jackson split third but Jackie also played some at first and second and in the outfield. Snider and Furillo were solid in the outfield.

We suffered a severe loss when Johnny Podres was called into the Navy before the season ever got underway. Since Johnny had come on so strong in the Series, it was a tremendous disappointment to know there was no way he was going to be on hand for any part of 1956.

Then in the early days of June we lost Don Zimmer when he was struck alongside the cheekbone by a fast ball thrown by Hal Jeffcoat (then with Cincinnati). Don just froze and we all felt sick when the ball smashed in with that dull, crushing sound.

Ultimately it was discovered that Zimmer's cheekbone was fractured. I was worried about his future because I remembered that in 1953 when he was with St. Paul he sustained a fractured skull. But Zimmer came back and never showed the slightest sign of fear, staying in the big leagues until closing out his career with Washington in 1965. Don only appeared in seventeen games for us that year and I've always felt those two incidents must have some way curtailed his career.

The 1956 season was almost a complete turnaround from 1955's flying start and early wrapup of the league title. This year the race was tight all the way, in fact, a five-team chase until the early days of July.

Finally it came down to a race between Milwaukee, Cincinnati and us. By the end of the season we had led the National League for a total of only about seventeen days at various times. You almost had to read the standings every morning to see who was in front. The biggest lead we ever enjoyed was 1½ games way back in the first month—April 28, to be exact.

The race wasn't settled until the final day, but there were many who insisted we won the pennant that year on May 15. The win didn't come on the field but in a trade. On the cutdown day to twenty-five players, we acquired Sal (The Barber) Maglie in an interleague purchase from Cleveland. Maglie got his nickname from his heavy black beard, as well as the fact that he had been a barber at one time in Niagara Falls.

Cleveland had placed him on the waiver list to meet the midnight cutdown. We remembered Sal well from his years with the Giants, especially 1951 when he was 23 and 6 and had a 2.93 earned run average. Sal was 18 and 4 in 1950 when he led the league in winning percentage at 81.8, and in 1952 he was 18–8. In 1954 when he helped beat us for the pennant he was 14 and 6.

We were short a pitcher with Podres' loss to the Navy, and even though to that point in time Maglie hadn't won a game with the Indians, our reports indicated his arm was solid and there was no question of his savvy or courage. Everyone in the organization considered it a wise move, not even a gamble, although he had turned thirty-nine on April 26. A man with his lifetime record and pitching credentials was almost sure to have that old right arm revitalized by a change in uniform.

It was. Sal posted a 13–5 record and a 2.89 ERA with us, but, most important, he was a great inspiration to everyone on the club that had once been his rival. All of his wins were big in the seesaw race we were in.

One of Sal's biggest wins came in the closing month of the

race when he went out against Bob Buhl of Milwaukee on September 11. This righthander had beaten us seven games in succession. Sal stopped his streak with a 4–2 win that put us in a tie with the Braves, the first time we had been in first place since April 28.

But Sal's big day in the National League race was still ahead. On the afternoon of September 25 Milwaukee beat Cincinnati. We had to beat Philadelphia that night to stay on their heels.

Not only did he beat the Phils but he did it with a brilliant 5–0 no-hitter. Quite an accomplishment for a man who was five months past his thirty-ninth birthday and locked in one of the tightest pennant races in National League history.

We were still in trouble the next day when, with only three more games to play, Robin Roberts beat Don Newcombe.

On September 28 we had a doubleheader against Pittsburgh. Once again Maglie came through with a win and Clem Labine got the other. Then that night Herm Wehmeier, who had not been too consistent over the years for Cincinnati, pitched for St. Louis against the Braves and beat them in a tight 12-inning game, 2–1. That gave us a game lead, and when we closed out the season on Sunday the pennant was ours by a game.

Once again we were in the World Series against the Yankees. They'd had an easy time in the American League. They took the lead on May 16 and were never headed, beating Cleveland by nine games.

This was one Series where we had no leeway to adjust our pitching staff. We were in a war to win the National League pennant right to the wire and had worked our tails off to come out on top. If the theory that a club with momentum was the best for a Series we had that.

We didn't have anyone who had hit for a big average. In fact, Jim Gilliam was our only regular who hit .300, and he was exactly on the figure. We got a little edge with power, primarily from Duke Snider, who ended up hitting .292 but led the league in home runs with 43, was fourth in RBIs at 101 behind Stan Musial's 109; was second in home run percentage at 7.9; was fourth in doubles with 33; the leader in slugging average at .598; second in total bases to Hank Aaron at 324; led the league in walks at 99 and at 112 was second in runs scored only to Frank Robinson's 122.

Campanella, whose bad hands hurt him all year, hit only .219 but he had 20 home runs and 73 runs batted in. Carl Furillo hit .289 but had 21 home runs and 83 RBIs. Hodges, with a .265 average, had 32 home runs and 87 RBIs. Even Sandy Amoros, whom you wouldn't call a real long-ball power hitter, batted .260 but had 16 home runs and 58 RBIs.

The Series opened in Brooklyn and Ebbets Field naturally was packed. Not only was it the Yankees against the Dodgers but Mr. O'Malley had invited President Eisenhower to come up from Washington for the first game. He threw out the first pitch and Campy caught it.

Although Newcombe had won 27 games for us to lead the National League, I decided to go with Maglie. The Old Man was superb, winning 6–3 and striking out ten. Maglie had asked me to pitch although he had only three days' rest. That wasn't really a concern because Sal had pitched in 13 games during the season with similar period of rest.

A lot of the Yankees, Billy Martin in particular, kept asking the umpires to look at the ball. But all Sal had was a sinker that really did its job mixing it up with what was left of his fast ball. It was a masterful game and the first win for Maglie in the Series, since he never won a game in 1951 with the Giants.

Maglie wasn't real loose for most of the game. I felt he really got his stuff about the sixth inning. I went to the mound in the top of the fifth when we were leading 6–3 to see how he was. Hank Bauer had singled, Enos Slaughter flied out and Mickey Mantle walked.

With two on and one out and Yogi Berra up I wanted to know how Sal felt. He told me he wasn't as sharp as he might be but he was confident he could get Berra. He forced Yogi to fly to Amoros and Bill Skowron did the same thing. That was the turning point of the game and once more supported my feeling that patience is one of the critical factors in managing a ball club.

The big question the critics were kicking around the next day was whether Sal could come back again with just three days' rest.

Big Newk, who had had so much trouble in the Series the year before, started game two. Newk had dominated National League pitching honors, being named Most Valuable Player and winning the Cy Young award. It's not often that a pitcher wins both of those. In both cases the runner-up was Sal Maglie,

Once again it wasn't Newk's day, and he took considerable abuse for his misfortune. That was a viewpoint I did not hold. Many insisted Don couldn't win the big games but when you win 27 games in the season as he had done a lot of them were big games.

New York bruised him pretty badly, getting six runs and six hits in one and a third innings. Berra's grand slam homer was the damaging shot. It sailed so far over the right field fence Furillo barely turned around.

We were down 6–0 at the end of an inning and a half, and there were quite a few spectators in Ebbets Field who had written us off. That wasn't to be either. We had a parade in the last of the second, scoring six runs to even things.

Ultimately we won the second game 13–8 in what then was the longest World Series game in history—3 hours and 26 minutes.

Now, with a two-game lead after two having been played, everyone was talking about the fact that only one team in history had ever come back from losing the first two to win the Series. That was our club from the year before.

The Yankees won game three when Enos Slaughter, a year older than Maglie, was the big factor, rapping out a long three-run home run in the sixth to beat us, 5–3. Casey Stengel had acquired Slaughter on August 25 from Kansas City for the $10,000 waiver price. In order to pick him up, however, they had to release Phil Rizzuto, an all-time Yankee great.

Ford pitched that victory and the next day Tom Sturdivant beat us, 6–2, thanks to a couple of home runs by Mantle and Bauer. That evened things up. This game marked the appearance of a 20-year-old right-hander for us who was going to be heard from. Don Drysdale, in his first year in the majors, worked the last two innings, allowing two hits and two runs. One of them was just a bit of frosting on the New York cake with Bauer's home run in the seventh.

I decided to come back with Maglie in game five. Stengel chose Don Larsen, a 27-year-old right-hander from San Diego who was 11–5 for the season with an ERA of 3.26.

It was Larsen's day. He had switched to a no windup delivery during the last two weeks of the season. We had had little trouble with him in the second game at Ebbets Field. But he had pitched and won four low-hit games during the final weeks of the American League season.

It was his day, his hour. Actually it was his 2 hours and 6 minutes when Larsen beat us 2–0. But more important, it was a no-hitter, and even more important it was a perfect game. We batted only 27 men and every one of them was set down. It took Larsen only 97 pitches to achieve an immortal niche in baseball history.

It's the first perfect game in Series history and the only one. In fact, it was the first perfect game in the major leagues since Charley Robertson of the White Sox did it on April 30, 1922.

We had two shots that might have shattered his no-hitter. Sandy Amoros hit one down the line in the fifth inning that was foul by inches. Then Duke Snider hit a long, towering foul in the fourth that just bent out.

The man calling the shots that day was Umpire Babe Pinelli. It was his last game behind the plate, as he was retiring after the Series. We sent Dale Mitchell up to bat in the ninth for Maglie. Mitchell was experienced. He'd been in a lot of pressure situations before, and he had a career batting average of .314.

Larsen was outside with his first pitch. Mitchell took a called strike, then a second one swinging. Larsen stepped out, turning his back toward the outfield. After stepping back in he cranked up that no windup delivery, and Pinelli's arm shot in the air for the called third strike.

The stadium came apart. Larsen was buried by his teammates and fans. That was what every one cared about—the no-hitter.

My concern was that we were one game away from elimination with two to play.

Completely overlooked in the bedlam and hysteria was Maglie. Sal had been superb in pitching a five-hitter, but his effort went unrewarded in the accomplishment of Larsen.

People said Sal pitched on guts, guile and determination. All of that is true. But he also had a lot of things going for him. He had good stuff and complete command but, most important, knowledge. He used his stuff well, mixing up his sinker, his fast ball and a breaking pitch. He was courageous and crafty that day, but almost totally ignored in the post-game reports.

We went into game six having to win. Clem Labine, who had worked in game four for us in 1955 against the Yanks, was my choice. Bob Turley, a fireballing righthander, was Stengel's.

What a matchup. Labine and Turley matched each other pitch for pitch. Labine had never started in the Series although he'd appeared in relief the year before. But he did a masterful job in a tense situation. Turley allowed us only four hits. Labine set the Yanks down with seven.

Clem won 1–0 in the tenth inning, thanks to Jackie Robinson and to Turley's wildness. Turley walked Gilliam. Pee Wee Reese laid down a perfect bunt to move him to second. For the second straight time Casey ordered Duke Snider walked.

That brought up Robinson. It was a second chance for Jackie. In the eighth he couldn't bring a run home but in this spot he did. He smashed a ball into left field that appeared headed right for Slaughter's glove. Then it just seemed to take off, soaring over his head for a single that scored Gilliam to even the Series.

Labine had been primarily a relief pitcher for us but I was confident that he could go nine and he did. For Clem it was a great win and it brought everything down to the final day. Another of those affairs with no tomorrow.

Actually there probably shouldn't have been a tomorrow. New York simply demolished us. Not only did they bomb Newk out with five hits and five runs after three innings but they manhandled four of our relief pitchers.

Newcombe had as good a stuff as I've seen him have. He either struck them out or they hit it over the fence. Berra got two two-run home runs and Elston Howard led off the fourth by putting his second pitch over the scoreboard in right field. That made it 4–0, and the rest of the nine runs were just window dressing.

Poor Newk was disgusted. He left before the game was over and got a lot of heat for not sticking around. There are two sides to such a situation and I felt sorry for him. People remembered those home runs in that seventh game. They conveniently forgot about Newk's greatness in winning 27 games to get us into the Series.

I told the club afterwards that they had worked like dogs all year long. They battled from behind and as far as I was concerned did a wonderful job fighting the Yankees right down to the seventh game.

My only real regret about 1956 was that the next day I couldn't head home to Darrtown. We were committed to make a tour of Japan. We left the next day amid a lot of bickering.

Carl Furillo flatly refused to go. Pee Wee, Jackie, Campy and a lot of the others didn't want to make the trip. I'd never been out of the United States before except to Canada but I hated to go more than anybody.

But we went. It was trying and tiring. We had a parade every day, long autograph sessions and beds that were a bit small. There was nothing but trouble throughout the trip. All of our brass was disturbed over the way we played, and at one point I was so disgusted and ready to go home that if I'd had the money I would have bought me a ticket and left.

I guess, after all, our feelings were too raw after the loss in the Series for us to be interested in an international goodwill tour. I am sure that each of us was very, very happy to get home. I know Darrtown looked awfully good to me when we finally made it.

22

FOR LELA AND ME 1957 had a great beginning when almost on the eve of our departure for Florida our daughter gave birth to Kimberly Kay Ogle. Now there was a granddaughter to attract our attention as well as a grandson and it made life just that much more wonderful.

Kim was born on February 23, and two days before that, word was released in Brooklyn that Mr. O'Malley had purchased the Los Angeles Angels of the Pacific Coast League from

P. K. Wrigley and the Chicago Cubs. That in itself wasn't unusual, but the Dodgers also acquired Wrigley Field in Los Angeles for a reported purchase price of $3,000,000.

Immediately all of baseball exploded. They knew that Mr. O'Malley had been trying for years, unsuccessfully, to get a new park in Brooklyn to replace Ebbets Field. Rumors flew thick and fast, and, of course, when we all assembled in Vero Beach, Mr. O'Malley, Bavasi, Fresco Thompson and our other executives spent more time being interviewed about moving than baseball.

"It is my considered opinion," Mr. O'Malley said time and again, "that Los Angeles will have major league baseball by 1960."

On March 4 a throng of Los Angeles sportswriters appeared in Vero Beach to await the arrival the next day of an official delegation headed by Los Angeles Mayor Norris Poulson. A little hint of the future came in a press conference.

"The next step for major league ball in Los Angeles," O'Malley told the California writers, "can come soon—very soon."

After his meeting with the mayor and other Los Angeles elected officials and civic leaders, they indicated their high optimism that the Dodgers would be changing names and soon.

"I'll take the edge off that right now," Mr. O'Malley said, but with a smile. "At this time there is nothing sufficiently final for our consideration. We got to know each other. The Dodgers are still in Brooklyn and Jersey City."

The latter referred to the fact that Mr. O'Malley, in trying to impress on Brooklyn the problem with our park, had taken some games to the Jersey City stadium across the river. There were only a few—perhaps ten as I recall—but it created quite a stir. There was lots of talk about park sites but not much action.

Every day there seemed to be a new rumor. Each time we moved to a city in Florida for an exhibition game a new batch of writers would add to the growing speculation. And as we played our way north it was the same story.

Shortly after the season opened in April there was another big development when attorneys for the club in Los Angeles filed articles of incorporation for the California Baseball Club, Inc. Mr. O'Malley went to Los Angeles late in April and on May 1 made an inspection tour of what the papers called his "local baseball interests." Now the talk around the office was that we might play some exhibitions in Los Angeles in 1958, possibly before the season and probably in the Coliseum.

"If the Dodgers come," Mayor Poulson said after Mr. O'Malley's visit, "they'll come next season."

There were no ifs, ands or buts as far as Los Angeles was concerned. New York was in a state of shock because all the talk of moving included taking the Giants to San Francisco. Fans were irate. The politicians in both boroughs were scrambling to keep the clubs, and some were screaming about "organized piracy" by officials from Los Angeles and San Francisco.

The shift of the two clubs was getting more attention than the season. Once more the National League was a dogfight. Five of us were in and out of first place. In mid-July there were only 2½ games between the Phils in first place and fifth-place Cincinnati. We were only two out and in fourth place, and it kept on going that way.

The race in the National League went right down to the final two weeks. Then Milwaukee caught fire, taking eleven of twelve games. The Braves finally won it by eight games over the Cards and we were three more back in third.

Baseball had been shocked back on May 28 when the National League president—Warren Giles—released a statement: "If Brooklyn and New York request consent before Oct. 1 to relocate their franchises in Los Angeles and San Francisco respectively, the league president is authorized to grant it."

Then about midway in September we got the word we'd be in Los Angeles for 1958. That was assured when Mr. O'Malley sent Harry Walsh, then his legal counsel, and Sylvan Oestreicher, a club director, to finalize the deal with the City of Los Angeles.

The New York papers made a big to-do about Mr. O'Malley's statement on September 18, 1957: "The Los Angeles offer is generally acceptable to us." Even though he deferred notifying the National League for a few days the Brooklyn Dodgers were no more. Now it would be the Los Angeles Dodgers. The Californians on the club, fellows like Duke Snider and Don Drysdale, were very happy, but a lot of the others like Hodges and Campanella—men who had deep roots in Brooklyn or on the East Coast—weren't too happy.

126

It didn't really matter to me one way or the other. Darrtown was still home to me. The only real concern I had was that we were going to play in the Coliseum on an interim basis until the Dodgers could build their own park—in something I'd never heard of at the time, called Chavez Ravine.

Mr. O'Malley figured we'd be in the Coliseum for two years. I hadn't seen the Coliseum except on TV but when I saw a diagram of the proposed field and the short fence in left field I wondered what it would do to our team.

The first time I visited the Coliseum, I thought to myself we could put all of Ebbets Field down on the grass. When we came in after spring training in 1958, there were all the marks of a baseball park but centerfield seemed like it was in another county. Duke Snider took one look at the right field fence and almost collapsed. It was out so far you'd need to hit the ball twice to get a home run.

I remembered our last game in Brooklyn. It was September 24 and maybe we had 7,000 people in the old park. I remember a little left-hander named Danny McDevitt, up for the first time with the Dodgers, who beat the Pirates, 2–0. It was kind of tough when the game was over and Gladys Gooding, our organist, who went all the way back to Larry MacPhail's days, played "Auld Lang Syne."

Everyone had a tear or two in their eyes. Even though Ebbets Field was a bandbox in comparison to other parks and looked like a toy against the Coliseum, it held a lot of memories for everyone.

Not only were we losing those great Brooklyn fans but we had an even more tragic loss early in 1958 to all of us as a team, to baseball itself and to the world in general.

Roy Campanella, whose power shots in left field we were counting on to sail over that Chinese fence in the Coliseum, was injured terribly only days before we were ready for spring training. Roy was driving to his home on Long Island when his car skidded on an icy road and into a tree. That was January 28, 1958. Roy never played another game of baseball. In fact, he never walked again. He sustained a fracture dislocation of the first and sixth cervical vertebrae at the base of his neck and was paralyzed from the neck down.

All of us were shocked at the devastating injury to this fine

127

and remarkable man. Everything that could be done for Roy, Mr. O'Malley had done, but Campy has been in a wheel chair ever since. It's a mark of his true character that his spirits are still high.

I called Campy every chance I could in those long months he was in the hospital just to let him know we would not forget him. He had been looking forward to California and the warm weather but especially that short porch in left field that I'd told him about and he had seen diagrams of. It was built for him, but he never got to hit a ball its way toward that towering screen 250 feet from home plate.

If ever there was a year of change in baseball for the Dodgers it was 1958. We had a shakeup in our coaching staff with two old friends—Billy Herman and Jake Pitler—leaving. When the replacements were announced, Greg Mulleavy, a longtime minor league manager with the Dodgers, was elevated to a coaching spot. The other newcomer set my critics to talking.

Charlie Dressen, whose demand for a long-term contract cost him his job in Brooklyn in 1954 and gave me mine, was brought back to coach.

Everyone—writers, commentators, columnists and fans— said my job was short if the Dodgers began to lose in Los Angeles. Dressen was the Los Angeles type. It was his home. He knew the Hollywood folks and they wanted a flashy, flamboyant guy to manage.

I wasn't particularly disturbed at Dressen being hired. He was a solid baseball man. I knew he was loyal and wouldn't be after my job. There was no sense worrying about it, and besides I believed Buzzie.

"Charlie is being hired as a coach," Bavasi told the writers, most of whom were new to covering major league baseball. "He knows he can never become the manager. He has agreed to it.

"Now," Buzzie said, looking the writers over, "I want you guys to realize that Charlie's job depends on you. The first time any of you writes that Dressen would have bunted when Alston hit away or quotes Charlie on anything embarrassing to the manager—then Dressen is fired. It's up to you."

From a pure baseball standard, 1958 was a disaster in almost every respect except for attendance. We were never a factor in the race although we came west with many of the guys who had put us up there third or better every year since 1945. Leo Durocher had finished seventh with the Dodgers in 1944, but little did I know that was ahead for us in 1958.

When the year was over, that was exactly where we were —in seventh, 21 games behind the Braves, who repeated as champions. But we drew 1,845,556 in the Coliseum, and it was an unbelievable sight to see that huge bowl stacked with people. The fans loved Vin Scully and Jerry Dogget. Those two did more to educate Los Angeles to major league baseball than anyone else.

They tell me you could walk through the stands and never miss a pitch. There were transistor radios everywhere, all tuned to the game. One game on August 30 drew 78,672 against the Giants. That was more than double the number that could have made it inside Ebbets Field.

It was ironic that perhaps our most reliable battery combination in Brooklyn—Big Newk and Campy—never won a game for Los Angeles. Newk came out with us but he had lost six games when he was traded to Cincinnati in June.

Campy, had he been able to be with us, would have been the one guy on the team that would have appreciated that short fence in left even though it had the forty-foot screen that was called everything from the Wall of China to the Chinese Pagoda. Roy pulled about 95 percent of his pitches, and usually they were long, high fly balls that would have worn the fans out shagging home runs.

Snider was a true power hitter but to right and right center. The dimensions of 300 feet down the line and 440 in dead center were too much even for a talent like Duke. I'll never forget coming out one evening during batting practice to find Duke standing out in left field throwing baseballs. He wasn't playing catch with anyone. He was trying to sling one up and over the top of the Coliseum. I don't think he could have batted one out, let alone thrown it over unless it was in relays.

We had a little talk and I might even have fined him a bit, but I'm not real sure. I didn't object to his having some fun, but I'd already lost enough talent without having him throw his arm out trying something Paul Bunyan might have been cut out for but not Duke Snider.

It was a long season only because we weren't too much of an

artistic success. For, oh, how Los Angeles took to the Dodgers. There were movie stars everywhere. I don't know how many season tickets were sold that year, but I don't think Ebbets Field could have held them all.

I wasn't in the good graces of a lot of them as we were in and out of the cellar most of the time before finishing seventh, two games ahead of the Phillies. Almost every day—sometimes twice a day—there were rumors I was going to be fired, but Mr. O'Malley and Buzzie stood fast. I remember one day in midseason the papers carried a picture of me being hanged in effigy at a gas station in San Pedro. The owner made some remark about not thinking too much of me as a manager. I don't know how he was at pumping gas, but I can tell you one thing, it's a lot easier pumping gas than winning baseball games.

Buzzie brought all the speculation to a rapid end early in August when he announced that I had been rehired for 1959. That might have been the earliest new contract I ever had. Since I never worried about such things, I just can't say.

It sure shut up a lot of critics, but I learned long ago, way back in Portsmouth when I started managing in 1940, that all you could do was to do your best with what you had each day and plan for tomorrow. That's the way I've played it all these years and there's no way a guy as old as I am is going to change that now. But I did wonder a lot about 1958. I figured we'd have to do something to turn things around in 1959.

I'd never finished seventh before in my life. I didn't like it. I knew darn well that Buzzie and Mr. O'Malley didn't. For sure the players didn't and the fans and writers let me know they didn't so there was no doubt some changes would be made.

23

AS WE PREPARED for the 1959 season we made two winter deals that were important but hardly what you would call earthshaking. In one we acquired Wally Moon from St. Louis. Wally had tailed off from being nearly a .300 hitter for the four previous seasons to .238 in 1958. But he was an intelligent player and the deal, though unimpressive on paper, turned out to be a great one for us. We also acquired Rip Repulski from the Phillies to give us another outfielder.

To get Moon we had to give up Gino Cimoli but we all felt it was worth it. Moon always hit well to the opposite field, and even though he was left-handed, he might be able to zero in on that Chinese wall.

We made another change between seasons that didn't involve personnel directly but helped every one of us. Engineers were brought in to study the Coliseum playing field contours and especially the location of the fences. There had to be some adjustment to the right field fence or power hitters like Duke Snider would continue to be frustrated.

Finally the decision was made to bring the right field fence in from its ridiculous distance of 440 feet to 375. At the same time the dead centerfield distance was changed from 425 to 410 feet. The left field screen stayed where it was since the only way it could have been increased was by tearing out the concrete and removing the seats.

The alteration of the distance to the fence plus the trade of Cimoli for Moon on December 4, 1958 played a big role in one of the tightest National League races on record.

Most people really didn't figure the Dodgers as being a factor, especially after our seventh-place finish the year before. But I felt we had a chance. We could improve, I knew, especially if Drysdale and Koufax could develop and some of the other young guys in the farm system would arrive.

Pee Wee Reese, who had been in command of shortstop for the Dodgers since coming up in 1940, retired after the 1958 season. He appeared in only 59 games and never was the Pee Wee many consider one of the game's great shortstops.

So in the early part of 1959 we dipped in to Fresco Thompson's farm system for the first time and brought up a youngster named Maury Wills. Although he didn't take over shortstop as his own until the next year he did play in 83 games and hit .260. Maury didn't become the terror at stealing until the following year but his speed and his ability to reach ground balls others couldn't really helped us.

It was obvious from the first game that we were going to have to kick and scratch for wins, but we had the guys determined to win no matter what it took. It was never easy. This National League race was something else for tension. The fans really loved it.

We were drawing well but the real potential fan interest in Los Angeles wasn't realized by even the most optimistic person until one May night in the Coliseum.

Roy Campanella was able to leave the hospital now and Walter O'Malley—who had paid Campy his full salary of $50,000 in 1958—decided something had to be done to aid him with his hospital bills.

I'll never forget the Roy Campanella Night they put on that May 8. Based on advance ticket sales we knew there was going to be a big crowd, but when I drove in along Santa Barbara Avenue with Joe Becker, our pitching coach, the traffic was stacking up and this was still late afternoon.

The official gate count was 93,103. Vin Scully had to put out what they called a Sigalert in Los Angeles to tell fans who were coming to stay home unless they had tickets. Bill Nicholas, who was then general manager of the Coliseum, estimated 10 to 15,000 other people were turned away.

Campy had never played a game in Los Angeles, something I've always regretted. Most of those present had never seen him except on TV, but it was a sight to behold when he was introduced. Pee Wee came back to wheel Campy onto the field. The lights were turned off and at a given signal the thousands of fans lit matches. It was a touching scene for a great man.

The exhibition we played Casey Stengel and the Yankees that night was only a prelude of what was to come. It turned the town upside down. The roar from the walls of spectators was deafening and the attendance shattered the all-time record for baseball—the 86,288 in 1948 at Cleveland in the World Series.

1959 was a year when you had to keep up with the National League standings in the papers if you wanted to know where you were. It was a dog fight all the way, with the lead changing hands over and over. Up until the final month it was a four-team race among Milwaukee, San Francisco, Pittsburgh and us.

Two weeks before the season closed only a single game separated the Braves, Giants and Dodgers. With eight games left in the regular season the Giants were ahead of the Braves and us by two games, and we were faced with the difficult task of closing out the race on the road—a definite disadvantage to any ball club.

But we were scrapping. We'd brought up Roger Craig—who had tailed off after his great performance in 1955 and gone back to the minors—from Spokane on June 19. That's where Maury Wills had come from earlier. In July we had recalled Larry Sherry, a Los Angeles native and brother of our reserve catcher, Norm, from St. Paul.

We picked up one other reserve from our farm club in Spokane about midseason—Chuck Essegian, a Stanford graduate who had played a lot of football in the Coliseum as well as in the Rose Bowl. We had traded Dick Gray, an infielder, to the Cards in June for Essegian and a pitcher named Lloyd Merritt.

So with Moon and Repulski, plus the youngsters from the farm system, we went into the final nine days of the season determined to hang in there one way or the other and finish on top.

Those were the most hectic final days I've ever been involved in. We began our final road swing in San Francisco with a day-night doubleheader against the Giants. We won both games before two full houses at the old minor league park—Seals Stadium. Roger Craig beat John Antonelli, 4–1, and that night

Don Drysdale whipped Mike McCormick, 5–3. Meanwhile, the Braves were in Philadelphia and Bob Buhl won for Milwaukee. This left the Giants and Dodgers tied for first with the Braves a half game back.

The next day—September 20—Podres won over Sam Jones, 8–2, to give us a series sweep against San Francisco. Milwaukee again beat the Phils. This left us in front by a half game over the Braves with the Giants third, a full game back.

Now on September 21 we had to travel to St. Louis. Meanwhile, Warren Spahn scored his twentieth victory of the year at Pittsburgh, so now we and the Braves were in a first-place tie.

On the 22nd we botched one up pretty badly, losing to the Cards, 11–10, when we could have won it. The Cubs beat the Giants, 5–4, and when the Braves edged the Pirates, 5–3, they took over first place.

The next day Roger Craig came through in a big way, shutting out St. Louis, 3–0. The Pirates upset the Braves, 5–4, and the Giants lost their fifth in a row when the Cubs nipped them, 9–8. Now we were tied once more with Milwaukee for the lead and the Giants were two full games back.

All three contenders were idle and by now the White Sox had clinched the American League flag and were wondering just who they were going to play. The one thing certain was that they didn't have to have alternate travel plans since the World Series would open in Chicago. But you can be sure they were playing a lot of scoreboard as we tried to settle things.

September 25 we moved back into undisputed possession of first place when Gil Hodges hit a home run in the 11th inning to beat the Cubs, 5–4. The Phils edged Lew Burdette and the Braves, 4–3, and the Giants were rained out.

On the next to last day of the season in Wrigley Field, the Cubs took us apart, 12–3, while Spahn was beating the Phils. Again it was the Dodgers and Braves on top. The Giants stayed up there when Sam Jones threw an eight-inning, 4–0, no-hitter halted by rain in what was the first game of a twilight doubleheader.

Now we were down to the final day. It was possible that the National League could end up in a three-way tie if we and the Braves lost and the Giants swept their doubleheader. The National League office and the Commissioner's office were going

134

around in circles preparing for a threeway playoff if it materialized. It would have added at least four games before the Series—possibly six, if both went the full three games in the best of three series.

We got into the playoff potential first when we beat the Cubs, 7–1, to share some part of the pennant. The Braves made it a two-way act by beating Philadelphia, but the Giants ended the biggest potential confusion when they lost their doubleheader.

Things were set now for the third playoff in the history of the National League. Ironically, the Dodgers had figured in the other two, losing to the Cards in 1946 and to the Giants in 1951 on that historic home run shot by Bobby Thomson in the third game.

Now we were on to Milwaukee for the opener of the play-offs. I chose Danny McDevitt, a comparatively small left-hander, to start. A few eyebrows raised at McDevitt's selection even though he was 10–8 for the year. But Danny's career record of ten wins in Milwaukee County Stadium seemed to justify it. Fred Haney selected Carlton Willey.

Danny didn't last the second inning as the Braves grabbed a 2–1 lead. I went to Larry Sherry, and how he came through. He went the rest of the way against Milwaukee, shutting them out and allowing only four hits. Norm Larker was instrumental in both our early runs and then John Roseboro put it away with a home run for a 3–2 victory.

Now we had gone from Chicago to Milwaukee and played the next day and here we were flying west to Los Angeles, where we were going to play a late afternoon game as the second in the best-of-three series.

It was a tense, marathon event that kept the 36,528 in the Coliseum edgy all the way. The game lasted four hours and six minutes. Twenty of our available forty-two players and six of our eleven pitchers were in the game that wasn't decided until the 12th inning.

We were in bad shape most of the way. Lew Burdette, one of the most crafty and skilled pitchers in the game at the time, was in front, 5–2, as we came up for our last at-bats in the ninth. There wasn't one of us who wanted to go back to Milwaukee for a third game. But then just as Burdette had been in total command he suddenly lost it.

We got successive singles from Moon, Snider and Hodges. Now the bases were full. No one was out. Haney decided to bring in the Braves top relief man, Don McMahon, to face Larker.

He was tough, but Larker lashed one of his fast balls off the Chinese wall in left to score two runs and move Hodges to third. Now the Braves were leading by a run, 5–4, and Haney—knowing there was no tomorrow—brought in Warren Spahn to pitch to Roseboro.

I countered by replacing Roseboro with Carl Furillo, who hadn't played much this season, appearing in only fifty games. But he knew Spahn well and was tough in a tight situation. Carl, as I recall, at thirty-seven was the only current Dodger who had appeared in the previous playoffs in 1946 and 1951.

Furillo was more than a match for Spahn. He ripped one deep into the right field corner that Hank Aaron really had to go all out to get, but the long sacrifice did the job, scoring Hodges and tying us at 5–5.

Both of us filled the bases in the eleventh but neither could score. In the last of the twelfth Bob Rush—the fifth Milwaukee pitcher—had two out. Hodges walked on a 3 and 1 pitch. Joe Pignatano, working behind the plate for Roseboro, singled down the third base line past Eddie Mathews but because the left fielders were in so close due to the shallow fence in the Coliseum Hodges had to hold at second.

Once more it was Furillo. He took a strike. Then Rush threw one of his fast ones in on the plate but Carl ripped it foul. On the next pitch Furillo laced the ball past the pitcher's box, just to the right of second. Felix Mantilla, who had shifted to short when Johnny Logan was hurt in the seventh, flagged the ball down behind the base. But he hesitated long enough to hold Hodges at third, then had no play at second and had to throw hurriedly to catch Furillo. The peg was low to Frank Torre, skipping past his glove, and Hodges raced home to score. We mobbed Gil at home and those in the Coliseum and the rest of Los Angeles went crazy.

It seemed like all the fans had their transistors on Vin, because when the roar had died down you could hear him say, "And it's on to Chicago for the World Series."

Los Angeles was so captivated by the Dodgers that year they

even put out a long-playing record of the great games and big moments with Vin and Jerry. Los Angeles had its first pennant in only its second year. For the Dodgers it was the tenth Series, and I was going into my third.

It was a strange race. We won only 88 games, a record low for a National League champion, and for the first time in five years Casey Stengel and the Yankees were not in the Series. That was a considerable disappointment to a lot of Los Angeles fans who knew Casey well but New York had finished third, 15 back of Chicago. They won by five over the Indians.

We felt like a bunch of zombies. It seemed as if we had been traveling for weeks and the next day we had to board the plane and fly out to Chicago. That was our rest. We played like zombies too in the first game, getting bombed out 11–0. Afterwards Gil Hodges said, "You hate to take a beating like that but the guys aren't down. We still have our confidence."

Despite the horrendous thumping there was a bright side. Johnny Klippstein and Sandy Koufax looked good in relief. I told the writers afterwards that Sandy might get a start in the Series some place.

We had a new face among the writers for that first game in Chicago. This fellow happened along when Al Lopez and I were visiting.

"I have no comment to make," was Lopez's reply to a question.

When the writer turned to me I gave him an equally dull answer. "Everything I say to you is off the record."

"It's just as well," this crusty old writer said. "I broke my pencil on the way to the park."

The writer was Casey Stengel, covering the Series for any by-play or banter Lopez and Alston could come up with. He was a classic man, and baseball's just not going to be the same with him gone.

No one would ever have called the '59 Dodgers a power team because we relied a great deal on speed. In fact, we led the National League in stolen bases with 84 and in fielding with a .981 average. But we won game two of the Series with power, thanks to Charlie Neal and the young outfielder we had acquired during the season, Chuck Essegian.

Johnny Podres was the winner of record in the 4–3 victory

137

that evened the series and sent us back to Los Angeles. John got a big assist from Larry Sherry, who worked the final three innings, allowing three hits and a run.

Actually, Podres ran a risk of not being the pitcher of record because when I had to pull him in the seventh he was trailing by a run. But the batter for him was Essegian and he smashed Bob Shaw's 3 and 1 pitch deep into the seats of the upper deck in left field to tie the score. Charlie Neal won it moments later with another homer.

There was no doubt in my mind about taking Podres out for a batter. There was no doubt about Essegian being the batter. We needed a long ball and Chuck had won several games for us in the clutch. So he was my choice over Furillo or Don Demeter.

It was quite a ride back to Los Angeles, but I don't think any of us were really ready for the welcome we got at International Airport. When our United Airlines DC-7 rolled up to unload and I looked out the window, there was the biggest crowd I'd ever seen waiting for us.

The newspapers said there were 5,000 or so. It sounded like 50,000. There were banners, bugles and cheers. "Dodgers too hot to handle," said one banner. "Darn the Sox," said another. "You're the Greatest," another.

We knew Los Angeles was excited over our winning the pennant but we'd had to leave town so soon we weren't really aware how excited. The rally left no doubt. It took us an hour or so just to clear the crowd.

The intensity of interest hit me with full impact that night as I read the paper. An article in the *Times* reported that the $10 box seats were bringing $120 each for the block of three tickets; $7 seats were going for $90 for the three and $4 reserved were bringing $35 for the set.

My phone wasn't listed but I had nothing but calls for tickets. I wondered about that since the Coliseum seated over 92,000 and that was about three times the capacity of Ebbets Field. Red Patterson, the Dodger publicity man for years and one of my closest friends, warned all of us to get to the Coliseum early. Not only was it going to be a big crowd, but Ringling Brothers Circus was playing a matinee and traffic was going to be very congested.

All the warnings couldn't have helped. Exposition Park, where the Coliseum is located, has large expanses of green grass and they were covered with picnic blankets, people and kids. No one could visualize the sight of the Coliseum packed on a warm October afternoon. When John Ramsey announced the attendance of 92,294—a World Series record—there was no doubt that the city's love affair with the Dodgers was for real.

We won game three, 3–1, behind a fine effort by Don Drysdale, who had recorded his best year to date, 17–13. Furillo broke up quite a duel between Drysdale and the White Sox pitchers with a pinch single in the seventh inning that scored Neal and Larker.

Drysdale showed what was to come from him. He was behind 3 and 2 against nine different batters, but every time managed to come in with the big pitch and get out of trouble. Once again Larry Sherry helped out, showing his class in the ninth inning as he struck out Norm Cash and Luis Aparicio. After Nellie Fox got his third single, Larry struck out Jim Landis to end it and the Dodger fans went crazy as we led, two games to one.

Those fans paid a gross gate of $549,071.76, by far the largest in Series history. It shattered the previous record by more than $69,000. That had been set in the fifth game at Cleveland in 1948 at $480,085.64.

There was quite a bit of second-guessing when I elected to use Furillo as the pinch hitter in the seventh with Duke Snider on the bench. I wanted Carl because we just needed a single and he had gotten a lot of base hits without striking out too often. There was no debate, though for a second or two I wasn't sure he'd gotten a hit. I thought Aparicio had it, but the ball just kind of hopped over his glove.

One thing that first game confirmed. That was my fear of what the huge crowd would do to everyone. The background was tough for almost everyone with all the white shirts flapping around. It was hard for a batter to pick up the ball and just about as hard for the fielders. In the eighth inning of the game Wally Moon lost an easy fly that just fell in front of him. Wally told me he never saw it leave the bat, and before he could find it among the crowd it was too late.

It was that way in every game. Each time the crowds were

larger and so were the gate receipts. We won the fourth game when Hodges smashed a tie-breaking home run and Larry Sherry relieved once more. Hodges's shot came off Staley as the lead-off man in the eighth.

Sherry, who had gone to Fairfax High in Los Angeles, was credited with the win, reducing his ERA to 1.29. The local fans loved Larry's work and we sure did.

Ahead 3 games to 1 and needing only one more, I decided to go with Sandy Koufax in game three in the Coliseum. Sandy had shown signs of greatness during the season when he tied Bob Feller's major league strike-out record at 18, and he'd provided fine relief in the Series.

We lost the third game in the Coliseum before another record crowd, but it wasn't Sandy's fault. We couldn't get him a single run, falling 1–0 on a three-man shutout pitched by Bob Shaw, Billy Pierce and Dick Donovan.

It was a game of misses as far as the Dodgers were concerned. Hodges and Neal barely missed on home runs over the screen. Jim Rivera, put into the game that inning by Al Lopez for defensive purposes, shagged down a shot by Neal that would have scored two runs.

We could have closed it out with a break here or there, but that's baseball. We'd had our share or more, as I look back on it. Both clubs played a great game but Chicago got a run on Lollar's double-play ground ball that scored Fox.

Lopez had made the right move putting Rivera in. I don't think anyone else on that club could have caught Neal's drive.

I knew after the first game that things would be tight in the Coliseum games. I thought there would be few runs and real close scores because everyone would be bothered by the crowd background.

Some questioned my use of Koufax. I never did. Sandy did a fine job. Though I saw him throw harder in later years, he wasn't wild this day and he had good stuff. I figured we were ahead either way. If he had won, the Series was over. As it was, Podres had an extra day's rest and he would be pitching in that big park in Chicago.

While Podres didn't come out the winner in our final victory to clinch the Series, he did the job. Sherry came in behind John after three and a third innings and went the rest of the

140

way, shutting out the White Sox and being recorded as the winning pitcher. He was tremendous, and he had been tremendous ever since he came up, having reeled off seven straight wins at one point in the season. In the Series he was incredible, a vital part of a tremendous team effort.

I said then and many times since that the 1959 World Champions may not have had as much talent as others but they had tremendous desire—tremendous togetherness, as we call it now —and they never quit. The club came from behind all the time. It made me look good. Whatever I did they came through, so I couldn't guess wrong too often.

I really hated to take Podres out of that game, but he was getting wild, usually the tipoff a pitcher was tired. I'd like to have had him close it out as a winner but the most important thing was to win and I couldn't take a chance. I had to go to Sherry, and it was the right move.

I almost goofed in the ninth when I sent Chuck Essegian out to bat for Snider. I thought the lefthander (Billy Pierce) was staying in. Then Al switched to Ray Moore, a righthander. But Chuck made me look like a genius when he smashed his second pinch hit home run of the Series.

We all felt great a few days later when they announced the winner's share at $11,231.18. But every man on the club made my job easier. Like Essegian hitting that home run. It was frosting on the cake since we were leading 8–3, but 9–3 is better and it made my mistake look right.

As I've always said about the '59 champions, they played like a championship team all the way. It was a manager's dream club.

24

LIFE AS MANAGER of the Los Angeles Dodgers was a bit different from manager of the Brooklyn Dodgers. While the pressures were the same and the demands during the winter following a championship season were almost identical, in other respects things differed.

Living in Los Angeles isn't Darrtown but it is more quiet and peaceful than Brooklyn. Lela and I have always rented an apartment in L.A., and during the years we played at the Coliseum we were out in the Baldwin Hills area. It was close to the Coliseum and I discovered quite a few things of interest in the area.

When I went with Lela one day to a shopping center to get some groceries, I noticed the Family Billiard Center. While she shopped I went in and watched them play pool. There were mostly kids, but up on a front table I noticed a nice, clean-cut looking older man playing straight pool. I watched them until time to pick up Lela.

The next time I wandered in the same man was sitting alone and I asked him if he wanted to play some straight pool. That's how I met Bill Thompson. He was a retired contractor, and we've played a lot of pool for four or five years. I liked straight pool and he preferred bank, so we alternated, and although I hadn't played much bank I became pretty good and we'd split most of those games.

After Dodger Stadium was opened we usually took an apartment closer to the ballpark, most of the time in the Los Feliz district about ten minutes away. About that time Bill moved to a mobile home park in the Saugus area. We get up there once or twice a year for a visit and a little pool.

142

When we start home after the season the Thompsons usually drive with us to Las Vegas for a few days. They're fine people and I enjoy shooting pool with Bill. Since we play every night after dinner in Darrtown I'm usually in pretty good shape. I can whip Harry, my son-in-law, pretty regularly. My grandson, Robin, isn't a bad player but the last few years he hasn't been around as much, since he's been going to college.

We made quite a few friends in the years we lived in the Baldwin Hills. It was a nice apartment house with a big pool in the middle and a double stack of apartments around it. Our first year there I met a fellow named Marty Angove.

We talked a lot and got to playing bridge together with our wives. Marty kept bringing up his ability as a duck hunter. He didn't brag but just kept telling me about how many ducks he had killed. We'd had a couple of duck dinners at his house and once in a while chukars.

He showed me his guns one time and especially a new Browning automatic he had just bought.

"Let's go try this gun out," he suggested.

"There's no place around here to shoot," I said, adding that I didn't want to drive a hundred miles or so into the country.

"Oh, we don't have to go that far," he told me. "There's a place east of downtown Los Angeles on Rosemead Boulevard called the International Gun Club.

"But it's one of those places where you shoot those clay birds."

Now I was interested. And when he asked if I had ever shot there I was honest. "No, I've never shot there. But I'll go along with you."

This was a beautiful gun club south of the San Bernardino Freeway and Marty was eager to test out his duck gun. It was a full choke, which would be all right for trap, but not good for skeet, where you need an open choke gun.

"I'm going into the clubhouse and see if I can rent a gun," I said.

When I asked if they had a Model 12 Winchester, the same type that I had at home and one of the best trap guns made, they said they did. I rented it and went out to where Marty was getting ready to shoot.

"You'd better go first," I explained, "so I can see how you do it."

He went to the number one post. Instead of hollering "Pull" he just said, "OK, let's go."

When he said go the trap boy pulled the release and out came the bird. By the time he got his gun to his shoulder the clay bird was out of his range.

"Hey," I told him, "as quick as they're going, I'm going to get ready."

So I got on the post, got the gun up and hollered "Go" just like he did. I knocked the bird down. Marty shot at five or six and never even knocked any dust out of them. By then I was bearing down a bit. My gun fit me almost as if it was my own.

I'd gone ten straight and was beginning to needle him about that expensive gun. I wanted to know where he shot those ducks we ate, or were they store-bought. Anyone could hit one of those slow-flying ducks, I told him, but those little round discs were maybe a little too tough for him.

I ended up hitting twenty-four out of twenty-five, while the best Marty got was five or six. I was all over him, teasing him and his gun something awful.

"Come on," I said, "let's go down there where they throw them sideways like ducks fly." He'd been saying he'd have a better chance if they were going across in front of him like ducks instead of straight out.

As we walked toward the skeet range I told him I wasn't too pleased with my gun and I'd like to try another. When I came back I asked the fellow in the shop if he had an 870 Remington, which is a good skeet gun and practically like my own except for having the short skeet barrel that spreads the charge out a little more.

I knew that if Marty had never shot skeet before he'd have more trouble than he did with trap. I broke twenty-three out of twenty-five and he ended up with four. He didn't quite understand why I should do so well and he so poorly. I didn't tell him for a long while but I could tell he was suspicious.

For a long time I couldn't get him to go out but he finally did and we've shot every year since. He's pretty good now even though I tease him all the time. He's quite an agitator himself and he's the first guy I call when I get back to L.A.

I love to shoot. I find it relaxing and I enjoy the competition, with everyone constantly trying to improve his score. I'm usually

Walter Alston residence at corner of Cherry and Apple Streets in Darrtown, Ohio. Walt's father, "handy with his hands," did all the bricklaying.

Walt's dad, also a skilled woodworker, completed many projects in Walt's well-equipped woodshop.

Family get-together (1962). On horseback, left to right: Grandson Rob Ogle and Trigger, daughter Dodie astride Abby, granddaughter Kim on Misty, and son-in-law Harry Ogle on Dusty. Walt and wife Lela are in foreground, with Walt's dad standing behind fence.

Kim, age 3½.

Walt's sister,
Dorothy Mae Tolley.

A happy moment. Newlyweds
Doris and Harry Ogle cut
their wedding cake.
(Photo by Dwight E. Dolan)

Pony Express. Rob and Trigger
will get the mail there in record time.

Mutual admiration society, man and horse. Smokey Alston and Dusty, his favorite five-gaited riding horse (Indianapolis News *photo by William Palmer*).

1965 Darrtown visitor Willie Mosconi gives host Walter Alston a few friendly tips (George Hoxie photo)

Awaiting spring training at Vero Beach, Walt and Lela Alston try to land a .300 hitter (Barney Stein photo).

Below: Two Walters, O'Malley and Alston, assess Dodger spring training progress (photo by Stan Wayman, Time-Life Picture Agency, © Time Inc.).

Another one of those hopeless discussions (Los Angeles Times photo by Neil Clemans).

Relaxing moment in St. Louis during road trip. Walt Alston (far right) gets ready to display his trap-shooting skills to (right to left) Dodger coach Billy Herman, pitcher Carl Erskine, and two Winchester rifle firm representatives.

Left: First year in Los Angeles. Below: Hail the conquering heroes! October 1959, at end of second Los Angeles season, delighted fans salute their returning Dodgers' World Series triumph.

Some favorite people. Above: During spring training, Walt chats with grandson Rob Ogle, working out with team, and former Dodger Gil Hodges, at that time New York Mets manager. Right: Tennis buff and favorite granddaughter, Kim Ogle (George Hoxie photo).

out at the club Wednesday, Thursday or Friday when we are home. Usually it's with the same four guys: Marty, who then had a part interest in Tidy Bowl; Jack Hudson, who is a retired civil engineer; and Jack Wolverton, who owns a couple of Volkswagen agencies in El Monte and Ontario.

That's the shooting gang, and we have a lot of fun. Then Lela's along just to keep us honest. Once in a great while she will shoot if we're short a man.

To show you what I knew about Los Angeles, I didn't even bring a gun with me the first year. But once Marty found that range I got my guns after the first road trip to Cincinnati and I've shot hundreds and hundreds of rounds every year since. I even have a small reloading rig that I store in the Dodger clubhouse between seasons so I can reload my shell casings. It saves a lot of money and lets you reuse the round five or six times before you have to throw it away.

Back home in the winter I do a lot of shooting at the Middletown Gun Club. That's up on the way toward Dayton. When I first started up there they had a pro—like a golf pro. His name was Bob Woods and he could break twenty-five in a row any time he wanted. We used to bet a dollar a round and I'd get twenty-two or twenty-three and once in a while go straight—twenty-five. He won more dollars than I did. Whenever he did, he'd go around the club waving the dollar and telling everyone he'd won some more Dodger money.

Figuring that Woody needed a little business to quiet him down, I never said anything about his waving that "Dodger money" around but one day when I got home from the club I went over to see Coxie.

I told Coxie what had been happening for the past four or five Sundays. Wasn't there something we could do to cut Woody down a bit, I asked him.

Now Somerville is about ten miles northeast of Darrtown and there's a little old foundry over there that can do just about anything you need done. I had brought a couple of clay birds home from the gun club. We ran over to Somerville to the foundry.

"Can you make any of these out of aluminum?" I asked.

"Well, sure," said the owner, "the next time I pour aluminum."

I was beginning to wonder what it would cost but I figured I was willing to go a little bit more than what it might be worth to put Woody in his place.

"I can make them for a dollar and a half apiece," he said.

"OK. I need at least ten or twelve. Make me a dozen of aluminum birds."

They turned out great. By the time we gave them a little paint job to look like clay there was no way you could tell the difference on the fly.

The next time I went to the Middletown club I didn't let on to anybody what was up except the trap boy.

I told him what had been happening. "We'll go shoot some practice now," I said, "and I'm going to try and work it so I get on the squad with Woody. I'll try to get on the post ahead of him. You find out where Woody is shooting, but be sure he is shooting behind me. As long as I don't miss don't throw him any aluminum birds. As soon as I miss one, you feed him an aluminum one. If I miss two you give him a second and so on."

I missed on nineteen. Woody was still straight and smoking them, laughing like everything at my miss. Here came the aluminum bird. He shot and I could hear the shot ringing off the bird.

Woody's a little hard of hearing to begin with and with the shotgun right beside his ear he didn't hear the shot ring off. From nineteen on I was straight so I had twenty-four. Woody had one more bird in his twenty-five. Out came another aluminum one and he missed. Actually he hit it but the aluminum didn't fall apart.

"I got some of Woody's money," I yelled in the clubhouse. We went out two more times that day and each time he got one bird less. He got busy checking his gun, looking over the sights, everything. I gave him a hard time going out in the field to gather up a few of them.

"Woody," I yelled, "I don't think you could hit one if I threw it up."

"Toss'er up," he snapped. He's kind of a bulldog type and was pretty hot.

I threw it up. He hit it but nothing happened. I threw it up again. He hit it again and nothing happened. A third time I threw it up, and now he was storming.

"What in tarnation is that thing?" he yelled. By now he knew he had hit it and he'd heard the shot ring off.

He picked one up and found out it was aluminum.

"You didn't say what kind of birds we were going to shoot," I told him, laughing like crazy.

We had a lot of fun out of it. I never gave him his three bucks back. They've still got some of those birds around the club. They made them into ash trays.

A few years back Middletown started The Smokey Alston Day Shoot. It's held at the club every February just before I have to go to Vero Beach to spring training. I've missed it only one year in the eight years it's been held. I've won it three times and finished second twice.

I'm not at the pro level like Woody but I can hold my own with most. It's just like playing pool. I am quite good, but if I play a guy like Willie Mosconi, which I've done a time or two, I may have a good streak but nothing as consistent as he does time after time. I've run over a hundred balls a time or two, but a pro like Mosconi can do that all the time and quite often can run off two or three hundred in a run. I think his record is around five hundred.

Back when I was playing ball in Rochester we had a player on the club named Steve Misrack. We played a lot of pool together before I discovered he was New Jersey champion for about three years. Steve used to referee some big pool matches, and it was he who introduced me to Mosconi. Steve's son is now one of the top ten pool players and better than Steve ever was.

One time when Mosconi was in Oxford giving an exhibition he came over to the house for dinner. After we were through we went into the room where my table is and played a bit. I opened the game by running off 47 balls. Now that's pretty good for me, but Mosconi came back and ran 154 before he missed.

He's an incredible talent and a fine man. I enjoy being around someone who is truly a master of his craft or profession. You know, a lot of people like a fine car and clothes, but I prefer fine guns and a good pool table.

Willie Mosconi gave me a gorgeous cue with his name on it. I'm real proud of that stick.

There's a special gun I'm proud of too. Back in 1955 the Winchester people gave me a fancy engraved Model 50. It has a gold plate engraved, "This 75,000th Winchester Model 50 is presented to Walter Alston by Winchester as Outdoorsman of the Year for 1955."

Our equipment manager, Nobe Kawano, has a cousin, Tad Kohara, who operates a pool room in Los Angeles and makes custom cues. A cue is mighty important to your game, you know, second only to the table, and it takes a time or two for you to get the right cue for your game. Of the three sticks Tad has made me, the third is the best. I don't travel around with it, though; I leave it home. Tad is an artist at making cues. I understand a lot of the pros are using his cues now.

We used to do a lot of horseback riding, but once Rob went off to college it was difficult for us to keep our horses in shape. Finally a few years back we sold them. By then I'd become hooked on motorcycles.

I'd see Maury Wills ride up to the park all the time on his big bike. I had always wished I had one but I didn't feel it was the thing to do. Actually, I suppose I was a little embarrassed to have one. I had ridden Maury's around the running track inside Dodger Stadium a time or two.

Then on Alston Day they gave me all those gifts like the Toyota car and a little trail bike. It was too little for me so I sold it for half price to Carroll Beringer, our batting practice pitcher then, and bought a Honda 175.

Riding around out in the country near Darrtown was enjoyable, especially in Hueston's Woods. After a while, though, I began to realize that the 175 wasn't quite powerful enough for what I wanted to do, so I gave it to Rob and Kimmie and bought a 350.

Finally I went all the way and got a Honda 500, a four-cylinder job with a lot of power and speed. It can go almost anywhere. I don't ride the major highways much, only the back roads out where you seldom see a soul. It's great.

A couple of years back when Rob was home for Christmas he kept kidding me about going for a ride.

"OK," I said, "I can stand the cold better than you. You'd better take the Honda 500, Rob, because it has a windshield that will keep you warmer."

We finally got them fired up. It was really cold, much too cold to be riding. After gasing up in Hamilton, we came back to Darrtown to ride the country roads west of the cemetery. That area has predominantly winding roads, but you can take the turns at 40 or 50.

We'd been riding a good time when Rob suggested we switch bikes and go home. It had turned dark and we were using our lights. Rob was probably a quarter mile ahead, when coming up a rise with a slight curve, I could see gravel the size of eggs on the road. Before I could slow up I hit one, and it threw me into the ditch. I fell off the bike and my head hit first, with my helmet scraping across some gravel and scratching up my left forehead. The bike was lying on my left leg and I couldn't get it off. Before I could put my foot on the seat to push it off I had to get out of my left shoe.

Once I was free I saw that the left turn signal was broken off and the cowling all bent and scratched. I was bleeding pretty freely when Rob rode up, once he discovered I wasn't coming.

When he was certain I was not badly hurt, he started to laugh and giggle, needling me about not being able to handle the big bike.

"If they know we had an accident," I told Rob as we were putting the bikes away, "they won't let us ride any more. You go in your mother's bathroom and get some of the bronze maekup stuff she puts on. I'll go in our bath to wash up and touch up my forehead."

That makeup was like putting iodine on raw flesh. Robbie got a big kick out of my squirming. It was a good thing everyone else was watching TV or they'd have wondered what we were up to.

We went in the living room. I took my usual chair. Rob sat on the divan across from me. But he couldn't keep from giggling, and the more he tried the more he giggled.

"What's so funny?" his mother asked. "What happened?"

"We were putting the motorcycles in the barn," I said, "and the overhead door came down before I was ready. It caught me on the helmet, knocked over the 500, broke the turn signal, bent the cowling, and scraped my forehead."

Next thing you know my eye had begun to swell and my face

was getting puffy. I was a mess. But they never knew until now what really happened.

There's nothing wrong with riding a motorcycle. It was my fault, living a little too dangerously, especially at night in the winter. It was a good lesson for both of us.

When the days are so bad I can't get out during the winter I either work in the shop or in my photo lab. I get a kick out of both. I've got hundreds of photos of Rob and Kim from the time they were tots until now when they're adults.

Sometimes I have to shuffle things around in my darkroom because I also load shotgun shells there. I do a lot more shooting of clay birds than film.

Winters are my time to enjoy my personal hobbies but when February comes around each year I get itchy. I'm getting ready to go to spring training.

There are people who wonder how I put up with travel and all the other tribulations of managing. They never stop to think that the travel part is something a lot of people pay a lot of money to do. I'm paid to travel and I enjoy it.

Managing I thoroughly enjoy as well. I've never felt better in my life. Right now I feel I can manage indefinitely, but the man who will determine that is Mr. O'Malley. When I took over in 1954 I knew I could do the job. I just played each day as it came, trying always to do my best and hoping the players would do their best too.

Sure, you feel better and you sleep better when you win. But there's nothing you can do about a game that is over. You can't change it. You can replay it as many times as you want but the score is always the same. All you can do is learn from it and look ahead to tomorrow.

That's why I look ahead to Vero Beach each year with such fond expectations. Baseball's a great game and a great part of it is spring training.

25

THERE ARE MANY fine things about managing a major league baseball team. But with the Dodgers they are better, because Mr. O'Malley does everything first class. We never have to wait in an airline terminal for a place. Our plane is there waiting for us. It's comfortable and well staffed, and that makes baseball travel much easier.

It's the same way in spring training. Thousands of people from cold country like New York and Ohio spend a lot of money to go south to Florida for a few days or a few weeks. We go south to Vero Beach every spring for free. But, we also work pretty hard for five or six weeks to get in shape.

In spite of all the work to be done, this is also a very relaxing time. We try to get in a little golf. I have no rules against playing golf in spring training. The only rule I have is that no one—and that includes me—goes on the course at Dodgertown before 3 P.M. I don't want some fellows who might have finished working out a little earlier to be walking by en route to the golf course while others are still working.

I see nothing wrong with golf. I do ask that the players walk so that will help their conditioning. And I've never been one who thought the golf swing interferes with swinging a bat.

A lot of the players bring their families down. Back when they had the old barracks they lived right on the base. Since new accommodations have been built, however, there aren't enough to take care of everyone, so rather than not have all of them, none are allowed.

The quarters are commodious. I'd not call them luxurious although they are that compared to the old Navy barracks. We have a little suite with a large living room, bedroom, and bath. We've occupied apartment 19 since the new quarters were constructed.

Everyone eats in a large dining facility about a block away. The building also holds the clubhouse and a large work area with a recreation room for the media. A lot of clubs have patterned their training facility after Dodgertown. For the past few years the New Orleans Saints have followed us in to train.

We have a nice little park named Holman Stadium, and the Safari Pines Country Club where we play golf is right next to it. In addition to the stadium we have three other practice fields, batting cages, a theater where we show movies every night, a swimming pool, tennis courts, shuffleboard, billiards and table tennis. It's just like a Florida resort.

The only problem is the fellows don't have too much time to play anything, except baseball. We start early in the morning and by 3 P.M. everyone has put in a hard day's work. I'm not a harsh taskmaster but I do want everyone to get in shape early.

One of my favorite people has been coming to Dodgertown as long as I have to take all our photographs. Herbie Scharfman has been coming to Dodgertown since 1949. He even has his own private darkroom next to the press room. It's a beauty. Every once in a while I'll get in there and confuse him bit. I'm always offering him free advice as to what lens opening to use and what shutter speed.

The Dodgers have one of these man-sized tricycles that Herbie uses to ride around the practice fields in. He can put all his cameras and lenses in the basket between the two rear wheels.

I needle him unmercifully about using that trike. One day one of the players, Steve Garvey or maybe Don Sutton—I can't remember—was riding a bike back and forth from Dodgertown to where he was living in town. I'd been on Herbie about the trike and when the player came by I asked to use the bike. I turned around and put my rump on the handlebars and went riding across the grass backwards. Well, Herbie snapped that picture, and I'll be darned if it didn't make the papers. I'd learned that trick as a kid in Darrtown but I'd never done it since I'd sold my bike. That shows how long something like that stays with you.

We have dinner every evening with the Scharfmans and we

have a dollar fine for anyone who complains about the coffee being cold or this not being right or something else not good. One night when I said something wasn't just right, Herbie collected the dollar. But he wasn't satisfied with just winning the dollar, he wanted it autographed. Well, I signed it but I wasn't going to let him get away with that.

It wasn't too long before I had my chance to get even. On the first golf course they built at Vero Beach you had to go over a little lake from the first tee. Herbie almost always hit the pond when we played it, and I told him he'd never get so he could make it. But one day I caught him out there practicing with a three-iron, hitting ball after ball across the lake. He didn't know I had seen him. One day he made me a wager of a dollar that I couldn't hit my shot over the lake and he could. We put up our money and Herbie teed up his ball since I insisted he had to go first.

"No, Herbie," I told him as he pulled out the three-iron. "Huh uh. I don't want to take your money that easy. That's the wrong club. Go with a two."

I knew Herbie hadn't practiced with a two, in fact, probably had never hit a two-iron in his life. His two-iron looked brand new. So he took the two-iron out and put the three back.

"Hold it," I said as he started to address the ball. I took the two dollar bills and laid them out on the grass nice and flat in front of the tee where his ball was resting. "Now swing."

Herbie takes the two-iron back, brings it forward, and you can see the way it's coming he's going to top the ball and dribble it into the lake.

The ball went eight feet. Right in the water.

I grab the two dollars and take off.

"Wait a minute, Walter," he yells. "Wait a minute."

When I get about a hundred feet away I turn around. He's got the three-iron out and clears the lake easily.

I've got his two bucks, but to this day he carries my autographed dollar around in his wallet.

Lela and the coaches' wives enjoy Vero. They do a lot of shopping. Lela does quite a bit of fishing in the Indian River and some of the lakes around. When Kim comes down they play a lot of golf.

Annually, spring training is a case of questions and answers.

Who is going to come up from the minors to stick with the Dodgers? Who is suddenly going to find himself and become great?

We'd had one young man like that whom we had been watching and waiting for since we signed him in 1955 in Brooklyn. Each year we thought he'd find everything and rise to greatness. No one wanted that more than the young man himself—Sandy Koufax.

If ever patience paid off, it was in Sandy's case. Not only his own patience but mine and that of everyone associated with the Dodgers. I had been present in Ebbets Field when Sandy worked out before we signed him. I knew he was wild, but he could throw a baseball with a velocity few could.

I recommended we sign him. "This guy's got a great arm and good stuff," I told Buzzie and the others. "Go ahead and sign him." The next spring—that would be 1955—he came to spring training with the Dodgers. Under the rule then in effect, as a bonus player he had to stay with us.

I watched him warm up behind the dining room the first day with another pitcher. They were just lobbing the ball back and forth—maybe forty to fifty feet between them. And Sandy just couldn't hit him with it. I thought to myself, what have we got here.

And it didn't get better for four or five years. You have to give Sandy the credit. He stayed with it. Lesser men would have quit. Not Sandy. He tried and tried and tried. And we tried right along with him. We used him a lot but not very long. He'd get a lot of strikeouts but also gave up a lot of walks and a lot of runs.

He was 11 and 11 our first year in Los Angeles. I thought he was bringing it together a time or two then, but each time he couldn't seem to hold onto the control he needed. In the 1959 series when he gave us that good relief effort and good start, I thought he had put it together. But in 1960 he was 8 and 13 with an earned run average of 3.91. He had 197 strikeouts, however, and everyone who batted against him was fearful of his smoke.

Joe Becker, my pitching coach in those days, spent hours and hours with Sandy. They'd never give up. Then in the spring of 1961 we went from Vero Beach by bus for an exhibition.

Norm Sherry was going to catch Sandy that day and between the two they decided that Sandy wouldn't throw full out, but use more curve balls and changes.

It seems that from then on Sandy began to gain more and more control. His statistics for 1961 show he was on his way, with an 18–13 record. Soon he was the most feared pitcher in baseball.

There is no question as far as I am concerned that Sandy's stuff and his control and overall pitching ability were as good as any left-hander I've ever met or seen. There is no question that he was one of the greatest.

And on top of that a wonderful person—not difficult to work with and never a problem, although to hear some of the tales you'd think he was the center of one of my biggest run-ins with players.

That's not quite true.

One spring, and I can't fix the year precisely, a lot of the guys were missing curfew. Now, I never believed in curfews, but I was working for Mr. O'Malley, Buzzie, Fresco, and the Dodger organization, and they did. We all lived in the same old World War II barracks. Mr. O'Malley had the downstairs suite and Leo Durocher and I had the one directly above.

This particular night I was in bed reading when I heard some guys creeping in. It was 1:30 A.M. or so and there was a lot of giggling and carrying on. They were making a good deal of noise and by the time I got out of bed and into the hall I could just see Sandy and Larry Sherry ducking into their room.

"Hey, wait a minute," I said. "Let me talk to you."

Sandy was already out of sight as Sherry was going in the door. By the time I got down there it was locked. Now I wanted in there. Maybe I didn't give them time to open the door before I started banging with my fist. I hit the door a good lick and my 1959 World Series ring pinched my finger pretty good and the ring split. Now I was angry.

I backed off to kick the door in when suddenly they opened it up. I was concerned because Sherry had a towel or something wrapped around his leg. I wasn't sure whether he was hurt or acting like a fool.

When they finally got that door open I was pretty hot. They insisted they had gone out for a hamburger. I would have believed them except for the fact that they locked the door on me. I was in the frame of mind to take some of their money and I finally did, but only after having a talk with each one of them.

Once we got squared away that no one was hurt we all went to bed. And I say "all," because I pretty well woke up that whole barracks from Mr. O'Malley on down.

By the middle of the 1961 season we all knew Sandy had arrived as a pitcher. In the next four years he did things most of us just dream about.

He pitched the first of his four no-hitters against the Mets on June 30, 1962. He got another against the Giants on May 11, 1963, a third against Philadelphia on June 4, 1964, and on September 9, 1965, in Dodger Stadium against the Cubs pitched his masterpiece, a perfect no-hit, no-run game.

Baseball lost one of its great stars and greatest attractions when he retired in November 1966 after the World Series. He was not quite thirty-one and was earning well over $100,000 a year, but he pitched every game in anguish. You couldn't believe that if you looked at his 1966 record. He won 27 games, lost only nine, had a 1.73 ERA in 323 innings, struck out 317 and walked only 77 batters.

Sandy Koufax was unique. One of a kind. Other great left-handers will come along but they'll always have to include him among the greatest.

The Los Angeles fans sure feel that way. In a poll for the bicentennial celebration the fans voted Koufax as the "most memorable personality" in Dodger history in Los Angeles. They also selected his perfect game as the "most memorable moment" in Los Angeles Dodger history.

You'd need a book or two to recite all of Sandy's accomplishments. His greatest was himself. He worked tirelessly to achieve success. Once he did he was no different than the Sandy who came in to Ebbets Field in 1955 to try out. He was team-oriented, took coaching well and worked hard.

Baseball's a team game. Not just the nine guys on the field but the twenty-five of them. You need them all to win. Each one plays a prominent role although most of the fans aren't aware of what the lesser fellows do.

That's like coaches. They're mighty important to me. I've had a lot of them over the years. Some of them, like Leo Durocher and Charlie Dressen, created a lot of public comment when they were hired and a few times while they were working, but they did their jobs.

I've never had any particular favorites among the coaches I've had over the years. I want them to do their job. I respect them. I try to relay through my coaches as much as possible what I want done. I try to treat everyone alike. I like to joke and kid with all my coaches and to a certain degree with the players. We've always had a pretty good bunch of agitators as coaches. They get the dry needle out and get back at me from time to time. That's good. But they know when I'm serious and that's what counts.

Over the years Buzzie, Fresco, Al Campanis and I have given a lot of thought to having a coach up in the press box like football does. I think it would be good, but it would have to be someone intimately aware of our team, our limitations and our assets.

I think such a person might pick up little things we can't see from the bench, particularly pitcher's motions and that sort of thing. We'll never know, but maybe we could have shortened the control process for Koufax, for example, or for others with problems.

A lot of the fellows who have coached with me over the years have been career Dodger men. Buzzie used to like to bring a fellow up from the minors so he could qualify for his pension. It always worked out well. A lot of our coaches went on to manage —Preston Gomez, Danny Ozark, the late Lefty Phillips. Of course, fellows like Durocher and Dressen were managing before they became coaches with me.

They all had one thing in common. They were good teachers and hard workers, and that's all-important in something so vital as coaching, where we try to teach everything the same way from the lowest minor league level to the majors.

No one man or two men can do it all. It's a team effort, really an organization effort. A total system. And I think it works.

26

COURT HASSLES and construction had turned our one-year stand in the Coliseum into four. We finally made it into Dodger Stadium in 1962. We'd lost out in the late stages of the 1961 National League race to Cincinnati by four games and all our fans and a good many of the experts predicted we'd win the pennant in the stadium in 1962.

We came close. We tied the Giants, forcing things into another playoff in which we lost, two games to one. It was one of the most disappointing seasons in my career.

It was a year of problems. It was also the year the National League added New York and Houston in an expansion move. We lost Gil Hodges, Charley Neal and Roger Craig to the Mets. The Colts, later renamed the Astros, took Norm Larker, Dick Farrell, and Bob Aspromonte.

Now that was a good deal of experience but we were confident we still had the talent needed to do the job. A great deal of our hope ended on July 17 in Cincinnati. Koufax started against the Reds and lasted only one inning. His left index finger was numb, and though he had a 14–5 record with a 2.54 ERA to that point, he was never to pitch successfully again that year.

The circulatory ailment was known as Reynaud's Phenomenon. It caused a constriction of the artery leading to the left index finger. This decreased the flow of blood, causing numbness and cold. It also prevented Sandy from getting a grip on the ball and maintaining control.

He was out for the rest of the season for all intents and purposes. He did try to pitch twice in September but lost both games.

If you could have all the "ifs" in baseball, we probably would have won the pennant. Sandy was off to a spectacular start. He appeared to be a cinch to set a new strikeout record but for half of the season he wasn't available.

So even though Don Drysdale achieved a remarkable record of 25–9 and Maury Wills established an all-time base-stealing record of 104, we couldn't win when it counted.

All of our hitting died at once. With that we faded. We were leading by four games with thirteen to play but we couldn't buy the base hits we needed. Houston and St. Louis killed us down the stretch. On the final regular season day Johnny Podres and Curt Simmons of the Cards hooked up in a duel and John lost, 1–0.

Meanwhile, the Giants won their seventh game of their final thirteen and we were in another playoff. It was the fourth in National League history and each had involved the Dodgers. It was my second.

Our pitching staff was in bad shape—tired, beset with physical problems—so I gambled with Sandy. I knew it was a gamble going in, but if anyone could rise to the occasion it was Koufax. Unfortunately, the finger still bothered him and he'd been inactive a long time. He had to leave after two innings.

The Giants won that one, 8–0, but the next day at Dodger Stadium we won, 8–7, thanks to a final relief effort by our fifth pitcher, Stan Williams. The next day we went into the ninth inning with a 4–2 lead, only to lose it with a bases full walk.

There were more shattered players after we lost that game than I've ever seen. The players locked the clubhouse from the press. Not until Wally Moon, a solid old pro, came out to tell the writers the team didn't want to talk to anyone did they disband.

That was the year Leo Durocher was supposed to have second-guessed me in public. A lot was written one way and the other. I've always maintained that if you can't say something good then you shouldn't say anything. I'm sure not going to violate that now, not after all these years.

Shortly after the World Series I received an offer to manage Cleveland that everyone said I was foolish not to accept. It was a fine offer, for five years. It was closer to Darrtown but I had had thirteen wonderful years with the Dodgers and Mr. O'Malley had been more than fair to me. I passed just like it was another hand in our family bridge tournament.

You can't work for better people. Mr. O'Malley stuck with me through the thin years. I realized that. When we did win I never asked for a long-term contract or made any salary demands. In all my years I've only asked for a raise once and I got it, but I can't remember when that was.

All I know, I've been signing those one-year contracts every year, beginning back in 1954 when I got $24,000. My last ones have all been over $100,000. I have no complaints. I love the game. I love the Dodgers. You know, when you get up there in that kind of money, there's not much difference whether it's $80,000 or $100,000 that you take home.

I've got the best job in the world. Mr. O'Malley has never bothered me. I never bother him. If they want me they call me. I never go near the front office unless it is a meeting I'm called to, and seldom do Mr. O'Malley or Peter come to the clubhouse.

I don't have any office except here in the clubhouse in Dodger Stadium. I've never had a secretary in my life and I don't need one.

Baseball's my business and I love it.

There was the usual winter talk about our collapse with some critics intimating that our team didn't have the competitive heart. That teed me off. Slumps are baseball. Our problem was that everyone slumped at once. I must have gone over the season a dozen times during that winter. My conclusion never changed. I couldn't make those numbers come up any other way. We lost but we didn't quit.

There were writers and commentators giving out with those same thoughts about slumping in the spring but our guys weren't buying it. They came to play 1963 like it should be— a new year.

The most pleasing and helpful sign of the whole spring was Koufax. Off-season treatment of his circulatory problem appeared to be successful. His numbness was gone. It was the Koufax we had seen the first half of 1962 for the full season of 1963.

It was a masterful season for Sandy, with just a tinge of worry. Our hearts all stopped on April 23 when Sandy's arm went limp in the seventh inning of a game against Milwaukee which

168

we were leading, 1–0. After missing three pitching turns, Sandy came back on May 7 to crush the Cards, 11–1, allowing only five hits in eight innings, walking one and striking out five.

Sandy appeared to be all right. Then on May 11 his greatness showed itself again. He went out against the Giants to pitch his first no-hitter in Dodger Stadium. He won 8–0 and lost a perfect game in the eighth when he walked Ed Bailey. He added another in the ninth, walking Willie McCovey.

Koufax was something that season, winning twenty-five and losing only five. He led the league in wins, led the starting pitchers in winning percentage with 83.3 percent; led the league in earned runs with a phenomenal 1.88; led in strikeouts with 306 in 311 innings.

We played all year like a team on a mission and that was to win. Like every year, it was not a season without problems. And one of ours made the headlines simply because everyone who traveled with us and wrote was right in on the scene.

We didn't get into gear very well at the start of things. In fact, we were flirting with the cellar when we left Pittsburgh on a Sunday afternoon the first week in May. We had just lost. We were in seventh place. A lot of nerves were frayed, and when we got on a rather ancient bus, some of the players began taunting Lee Scott, our traveling secretary, about the quality of our bus, its lack of air conditioning and the fact the Pirates had just passed us in a new one.

Finally I'd had it. I told the driver to pull off and stop on the next shoulder.

"Does anyone want to take charge of the bus department?" I yelled. There couldn't have been any doubt in any player's mind that I was boiling.

The whole traveling party was along, even the writers like Frank Finch of the *Times,* Bob Hunter of the *Herald-Examiner* and George Lederer of the *Long Beach Independent Press-Telegram.*

There were no volunteers that I could hear.

"Then I'm in charge." I told Scottie that it was his responsibility in the future to order buses that were no better or no worse than any other club used. I told him to check with me in every city we stopped.

"If any of you don't like the buses I get from now on," I

continued and I was sure no one could help hearing me, "you come to me. Now if any of you want, right now, we'll step outside and discuss it between ourselves. And that goes for all of you."

There were no takers.

The next day Frank Finch asked me if that offer would have included Frank Howard, our giant first baseman outfielder who was as strong as a young bull.

I told Frank it didn't, that I was too old to fight. But I was so mad at that instant I probably would have stepped off that bus with Howard, and he towered a good five inches over me and outweighed me by about sixty pounds.

Frank was awfully strong. When he was just a rookie, I had challenged him to a little game I often play with the players. You extend your arms out with each of you getting a grip on one end of a bat. Then on a "go" signal you twist to see who loses his grip first. Of course, I turned him then. He wanted a rematch but I knew better than that. "You're not mature yet, Frank," I told him. "I want you to wait until you're fully grown and then I'll give you another tournament." Frank was always after me but I never gave him a second chance.

Another time in the Coliseum Jerry Lewis had a movie going involving a baseball team and a Japanese sumo wrestler. I was in this little skit as a manager, along with Pee Wee Reese and Gil Hodges. They were good agitators and they talked this 350 or 400-pound Japanese wrestler into bat twisting with me.

I looked at his hands and saw that he had strong but real stubby fingers. That was to my advantage. So was the fact he had never done it before. He really wasn't too tough and it wasn't much of a contest.

That little bus incident in Pittsburgh was blown way out of proportion but it did kind of pull us together. We went on to win the pennant by six games over the Cards.

Looking back on the standings now, I realize it appears that we had a little room to spare since we won by six games. The facts are it was a fight all the way. We lost only six games out of nineteen in September, yet we lost ground. St. Louis, under Johnny Keane, came on with a roar. They lost only once in twenty games.

When we moved into St. Louis on the night of September

16, our lead was one game. We had three coming up with the Cards. Podres gave us running room with a three-hit, 3–1 win. Then Koufax followed up with a 4–0 shutout. The Cards took a 5–1 lead in the final game, but a rookie first baseman named Dick Nen, just up from Spokane, tied it up for us with a home run.

In the eighth Ron Perranoski, who had one of the finest years any relief pitcher ever had, winning sixteen with an ERA of 1.67 in 69 appearances, came in. Ron had to throw six innings of shutout ball before we won it in the 13th, 6–5.

We left St. Louis four games in front with nine to play, and that's where the race really ended for the right to meet the Yankees in the Series.

Once more the Yankees minus Casey Stengel were heavy favorites. They'd won the American League by 10½ games. They had Mickey Mantle, Roger Maris, Elston Howard, Tony Kubek, Clete Boyer, Yogi Berra, John Blanchard, Whitey Ford, Jim Bouton and Al Downing, who was later to become a Dodger.

New York had won twenty World Championships. Six had been in four-game sweeps. It was an incredible Series—the first in Dodger Stadium, and that made the attraction even greater in Los Angeles, where tickets were harder to find than some of the freeway off ramps.

We opened in Yankee Stadium and I had written a piece for the *Los Angeles Times* in which I said: "I believe we will win the World Series the way we won in the National League—with speed and pitching. . . . I'm counting most on Sandy Koufax, Johnny Podres and Don Drysdale and, in the bullpen, Ron Perranoski."

Sandy started us off right. He fanned the first five Yankees, ending up with a Series strikeout record of fifteen and a 5–2 victory. The game lasted only two hours and nine minutes, and Koufax's record erased one Carl Erskine had set ten years before to the day.

We had acquired Bill Skowron, a longtime member of the Yankees, between seasons, but his .203 average and four home runs weren't too impressive. However, I felt the familiarity of Yankee Stadium would be valuable to him. It was. He went two for three, including driving home Frank Howard. And Moose, as fans loved to call him, played the whole Series at first.

171

Since the stadium was a left-hander's park Podres started game two and won 4–1. In two days, each of our fine left-handers had given us a big bulge as we headed to the west and Dodger Stadium.

There was another huge airport reception for us and the center of attention over anyone else was Koufax. The fans mobbed him. It was all we could do to get him out of the airport as fans reached out to touch him, shake his hand or get an autograph.

We went with Don Drysdale in the third game, the first in Dodger Stadium, and he was superb. He shut New York out, 1–0. Only two of those power hitters got to third, as Drysdale struck out nine.

Koufax and Podres were great but I think Drysdale was their equal at that point in time. He hardly made a bad pitch. His best ones were all at the right time. For instance, in the sixth inning with the tying run at third, he struck out Mantle.

I don't think he missed on a pitch all day. You can't do better than that. The only way he could have improved was with a no-hitter.

There was no doubt who would go in game four: Koufax. Ralph Houk, who had taken over the Yankees when Casey Stengel retired the year before, went with his best—Whitey Ford.

Some of the writers claim that New York knew it was over when they came to the park with their bags on the bus. Sandy helped them along by beating them 3–1 to close out a stunning four-game sweep.

Koufax struck out eight to give him a Series total of twenty-three, a new record. We did it the hard way, winning with only two hits. But I've never been one to worry about statistics if we had the most runs.

It was particularly pleasing for me. I knew our pitching was excellent but with the sweep it proved me an even better prophet. It was my third Series win as manager of the Dodgers and put me up there with some pretty important company. That tied me with John McGraw for the most Series won by a National League manager.

Koufax might not have been quite as sharp as in the first game but he had it when it counted. He paced himself well, and I wasn't about to remove him in the ninth when he got into a little trouble. He made two fantastic curve ball pitches that inning. One got Tom Tresh and the other set Mantle down. Both were called strikes. Those were terrific pitches.

Not only did we sweep that series in four—and no one figured that—but it may have been the fastest series of all time. Remember the first game took two hours and nine minutes. Game two was 2:13, game three 2:05 and Sandy's finale lasted only one hour and fifty minutes.

It was a pretty good series for our pocketbooks, too. Each full share was worth $12,794 per man, then an all-time record.

To illustrate how much of a pitchers' series it was, the Yankees set an all-time series record for a low team batting average at .171. We didn't set any worlds on fire with a .214 team average but we had all we needed.

We weren't there, of course, but folks tell me that Dad and the rest of Darrtown had one of the biggest celebrations of all time that final Sunday afternoon. When we got home, one lady fan allowed, "I've never seen so much activity since I don't know when."

27

OVER MY YEARS in baseball I've made a lot of friends among what we now call the media. It used to be the press but now radio and television are so big the name has changed. A lot of them have called me the quiet man—a reference I don't totally agree with. Maybe I am to some. Others might not agree. Everyone who knows me well realizes that I'm slow to anger but, once I boil—watch out, it's pretty hard to calm me down.

Some of the older Los Angeles writers remember the night

I broke my World Series ring in Vero Beach trying to get into Sandy Koufax and Larry Sherry's room. A lot of them were along in the bus that day in Pittsburgh. And there have been a few other times.

I've always tried to meet everyone halfway whether they're writers, players or whatever. If they'll treat me the same way, we'll get along real well. Some of my media friends like Red Smith and Dick Young go way back to my first year as manager of the Dodgers. In those days New York had a lot of papers and there were a lot of fellows traveling with us from time to time.

One of my big run-ins of all time was with a writer, one I didn't even know. But the way he wrote he sure must have known me. This was Maury Allen of the *New York Post,* and sometime during the 1963 pennant race he wrote the worst article about me I had ever seen. After someone sent it to me, I kept asking if he was around every time we'd get to New York. It wasn't until spring training of 1964 when we had gone to St. Petersburg to play the Yankees that he was pointed out to me.

I was sitting on the bench talking with Red Smith, Dick Young, Frank Finch and some of the other writers when this fellow Allen walked up and stuck his hand out. There was no way I would shake hands with him, and I told him so in pretty strong language.

When he asked why I felt that way I hit the boiling point.

"First of all," I said, and from my tone and tempo there was no doubt I was mad, "you don't even know me. You wrote a lot of personal things about me that you had no way of knowing because you've never met me. Thousands of people read it. Now there's a difference between us. I'm going to tell you face to face what I think of you. If you've got a gut in your body you won't stand there and take it."

But he did. Then I realized we'd attracted quite a crowd. I don't really like public displays and I wanted to avoid that but yet not give up my point.

"Now I'm going in the clubhouse," I told him, "and if you want to come in we'll finish our conversation."

I wasn't sure if he would come in, but he did. Then I wasn't sure if he was going to challenge me or I was going to challenge

174

him, but I was sure of one thing—I kicked off my spikes because I didn't want to be skating around on that cement floor in spikes.

"Everything I said outside goes. I still say if you've got a gut in your body you're not going to take it. I'm not going to take the first pop. I'm giving you that advantage, because you'll need that much edge."

The only others in the dressing room were Koufax and the trainer who was rubbing him down. But about then the door opened and in came Red Patterson, the longtime Dodger publicity man and my close friend.

Old Red is a diplomat. He kind of eased the guy out the door and I thought it was all over. But that story got more space in more papers than his original article, so maybe I didn't accomplish too much.

Bavasi and Red had always told me to make friends with the writers. Have a drink with them. Go out to dinner here and there. But I was stubborn. I thought if I had to buy my way into this thing, into their friendship to have them pat me on the back, that wasn't going to be. That wasn't my way. I would rather dig post holes or something.

Bob Hunter, who's covered the Dodgers in Los Angeles since the day we arrived, is always kidding me. "When are we going to have a drink, Skip?" he'll ask me. I keep kidding him along about next week just as I've been doing for eighteen years.

I don't like to drink. I get no pleasure out of it. In fact, it bothers my stomach so I kid Bob and the guys along and over the years we've become good friends.

Over the years a lot of writers have asked me who first called me The Quiet Man. I don't know. A writer, I'm sure, and probably a couple of years after I went to Brooklyn. I needled Red Patterson for years to do a little research and find out that answer for me instead of smoking all those cigars but he never did.

Red's one of my favorites. He was a sportswriter in New York for years. Then the Dodgers hired him away from the Yankees to do PR, and what a job he did.

Over the years I've relied on Red for a lot of things and he's seldom been wrong. He's a real fine person and the hardest

175

worker I've ever known. I was always on him and especially at meetings, banquets and places where I wasn't so deeply involved with trying to win a baseball game.

I remember the first year the Mets got in the Series. Red got into New York ahead of me and got us a suite together in the Roosevelt Hotel. It had an entryway into the suite about four by four with a second door.

It was about midnight, and Red was dozing off as I watched the news. The phone kept ringing but I wouldn't answer it. All the calls were for Red.

Red's head no more than hit the pillow and he was asleep. The phone began to ring again. As it rang the third time Red woke up.

"Skip? Didn't the phone ring?"

"Yeah, it rang, Red."

He started trying to get the operator to find out who called. He rattled the button for about five minutes. It was the night before the first game and the hotel was swamped. Finally he got an operator.

"Did you call this room?" . . . "You didn't? You're sure?" Red asked a time or two.

"Skip, didn't the phone ring here?"

"Yeah, Red, the phone rang but it was on TV."

Red was madder than a wet hen. He slammed his head down on the pillow. A few minutes later I turned off the TV, hoping to get to sleep before Red because he snores up a storm.

Five minutes later the phone rang. Red nearly knocked the lamp over, pushing the receiver onto the floor where he couldn't find it. Finally, he managed to get the lamp on. He picked up the phone and it was Peter O'Malley.

"Yeah, Peter, I got the tickets. How I'm going to get them to you tonight? Can't it wait until morning?"

Peter tells him he has to have them for these stewardesses who had been on the flight the Dodgers came in on.

"Tell you what I'll do, Peter. I'll leave them right inside the entry on the table. I'll leave the outside door open and they can come pick them up."

Now Red gets up, fiddles around with his stack of tickets until he finds the ones he wants, and goes out to leave them in the entry. I was lying there pretending to be asleep when I heard Red go out to leave the tickets for the girls. I could hear the inner door click closed, the outer door open and Red fix it so they could get in.

Then I heard a knock on our suite door.

"Skip?"

Another knock.

"Hey, Skip, it's me, Red. Let me in."

Now I knew Red had a problem. He sleeps sans pajamas.

Bang, bang, bang. "Hey, Skipper—" I just lay there laughing to myself.

Bam, bam, bam. "Alston! . . . Alston!! . . . Hey, Alston, damn you, Alston, wake up!"

Now he's using his foot kicking and kicking. I heard the elevator stop on our floor and the door open.

By now he was kicking with one foot, beating with his fist, and screaming. "Alston, Alston, wake up. Alston, I know you're awake, let me in."

"Is that you, Red?" I asked as I could hear women coming down the hall, reading off door numbers out loud.

"Let me in!"

"Where are you, Red?"

"You know where I am. Let me in."

"OK. Wait 'til I get some clothes on."

"No, damn you. Let me in now."

I opened the door and just about the time we closed it the girls opened the outside door.

I remember another time when we were at the Fountainbleau Hotel in Miami at a winter meeting. We'd had a sandwich and coffee and the bill was about $5. I think he gave them a 75-cent tip.

"Red," I said, "look at that headwaiter over there. He's pointing to you and complaining about the tip." They were looking at us and Red turned beet red.

The next day we had dinner and the bill was about $11.

"Now, Red," I told him, "don't be a cheapskate on the tip. Leave 'em a good tip."

"I'll teach you to make fun of my tipping," he said. He signed the bill with my name and added a $10 tip.

177

Red's the only vice president of anything I ever knew that you could pull things like that on and he'd come right back like it never happened.

In Japan on our first trip, he came in one day to have me make out the lineup card and handed me a pencil.

"Red, you can't write a lineup card in triplicate with a pencil. I need one of those ball point pens."

Red went off and came back in a few minutes with a Japanese ball point pen.

"Is there any coffee around?" I asked, knowing full well that tea is the national drink in Japan. But I'll be darned if Red didn't come back with some coffee. It was black coffee, which I always drink.

"Where's the cream?" I asked.

"You drink it black."

"No, I don't, not over here. I drink it with cream."

Off he went and came back with cream in it.

"Oh, Red," I said, shaking my head, "you forgot the sugar."

By then he knew he was being put on.

"Just fill out the card," he said, shaking his head and saying something I know wasn't polite under his breath.

You miss a guy like that although I'm happy that he became president of the California Angels just before spring training started in 1975. He's still a great friend, but I miss his not being with us every day. He was always good for a laugh and I spent a lot of time with him. As manager you can't show favoritism to any player so you are more or less left alone.

Over the years Lela has always made the trips to Cincinnati and maybe another one or two. But when Robin got to be ten or so he began going to spring training with us and on the road once in a while. Over the years I surely enjoyed watching him play catch with the various players, go hunting and fishing with Jim Brewer down in Florida, and learn from the experts how to play first base.

When he was ten or eleven, on a road trip with us that ended up in Milwaukee, I took him to the airport and got him on the plane back to Ohio. He wasn't the least bit concerned, giving me a wave as he went in the plane door.

Over the years we did a lot together—hunting, woodworking,

riding the horses; later on riding the motorbikes, shooting—everything a grandpa does with a grandson. It's hard to believe he's grown, almost through at the University of New Mexico, and a pretty good ball player.

It's really interesting to watch youngsters grow when you know them so closely. Rob and Kim are especially in that category since they're in the family. Peter O'Malley, now president of the Dodgers, is another. I remember when he was a schoolboy coming to camp with Mr. O'Malley. I watched him through college, then at various jobs such as being in charge of Dodgertown, and now he's running the ball club.

Peter does a great job. There's a lot of his father in him. He doesn't try to run the club on the field but takes care of the business end and lets Al and me and the rest of the coaches and scouts take care of the baseball.

You don't often get to see one of your players grow up. But we did in Steve Garvey's case. His father drove the bus for our road trips around Florida. Steve started coming along when he was ten or eleven. He used to ride quietly along, as all good little boys should be seen and not heard. We insisted, more or less, that Steve's dad be our driver. Steve finally became our bat boy on the road. The next thing we knew he was off at Michigan State playing defensive halfback and outfield in baseball.

Finally we signed him, and ultimately he found himself as a first baseman. In 1974 he became the most valuable player and the Golden Glove first baseman in the National League. You enjoy looking back at the youngster and seeing what a fine man he has turned out to be, a nice guy all the way around.

But baseball is full of nice guys. A lot of them have done real well for me and the Dodgers, as well as for other teams in the game.

There is no way you can put down in a few words the philosophy or psychology of managing a baseball team. I go into it in great depth on all aspects of baseball in *The Baseball Handbook,* a technique book I wrote with Don Weiskopf. It covers everything from tying your shoes to the finest points in strategy.

My philosophy of managing is rather simple. I believe in keeping everything simple, allowing a great deal of room for the individual to think on his own and respond within general confines we have set down for the whole Dodger organization. The most important thing in my opinion is to know your players. Know them as players in terms of their assets and liabilities, but, more important, know them as persons. That's where you determine how you can get the best from them. Most respond to a pat on the back. That's about 95 percent. A few you have to give a boot in the rear. That's the other 5 percent.

I've always told our players that I wanted 100 percent from them when we're playing baseball whether it be in a workout, an exhibition, a regular season game or the World Series. If they give me that we'll get along fine.

I remember the year we brought Maury Wills up from Spokane. He had his problems. Threw some balls away. Once in a while went streaking out for a ball that few humans could reach. He had a lot of pride and had gone hitless in the last few games and was disappointed in himself.

"Skip," he said to me in the shower after one game, "why don't you send me back to Spokane? I'm not doing you any good."

"Maury, if you have as much confidence in yourself as I have in you everything is going to be OK," I told him. "Just go out there and play your game." I had seen things in the way he moved, his aggressive desire, his tremendous speed and quickness that I just knew would all come together.

And, oh, how they did. After much frustration he taught himself to be a switch hitter. That enabled him to get on base more often than if he had batted right-handed all the way. His base skills he developed by tireless, hard work, and there is little doubt he is the greatest the game has seen.

To illustrate his total determination about everything, Maury decided in his final few years to learn how to play the banjo. He hauled that thing around all season long, picking out tunes until he got to be a darn good banjo player.

Just last year Ivan De Jesus, a young shortstop with a good deal of potential, kicked an easy grounder in an intra-squad game. He was very despondent at his play. "Don't feel badly," I told him afterwards in the clubhouse. "You played it correctly. You charged the ball properly. Whether it took a bounce or whatever happened doesn't matter. Don't feel badly about it."

I'm convinced that kind of response does more good 95 percent of the time than ripping into them, especially for a young player. It takes a lot of patience sometimes. It also pays if you are going to reprimand a player pretty hard to wait a day, then get him alone out on the field and go over the whole thing.

You have twenty-five totally different individuals out there. Each one of them is a high strung, highly talented, finely tuned man gifted with baseball skills or he would never be wearing a Dodger uniform.

You get a lot of free advice on how you should do things in player relations. It's been the same forever in baseball. But I think those of us managing know more about the player, his personality, his problems, and his health at the moment than anyone else. So I play it my way. If things go wrong I can take the heat. I've been doing it for a long time and it's easier on an old gaffer like me than one of the younger guys.

You know, there's a lot of boy in every man, and just because he's wearing Dodger blue doesn't make him different from the rest of the world. He just happens to be endowed with the great talent that God bestows on people in various walks of life. And the major league baseball player usually has received more than his share to be on the field.

28

AFTER TAILING OFF in 1964 and finishing sixth, thirteen games behind the pennant-winning Cardinals, we came back in 1965 for another of those typical dog-eat-dog, down-to-the-wire races that have been so characteristic of the Dodgers and the National League during my years.

During the early days of June we had a five-game lead but it lasted less than twenty-four hours and we never led by that much again. In fact, from then on the lead seemed to be handed back and forth among the Braves, Reds, Giants and us.

A great deal of our hopes appeared to be shattered on May 1 when Tommy Davis, who had led the National League in hitting in 1962 and 1963, sustained a fractured ankle sliding into second base and never played another inning. We had his bat for only seventeen games, and losing a quality player that early, it's difficult to replace him.

But we were fortunate, as we were all season, when we brought up Lou Johnson from our Spokane farm club. Now Sweet Lou, as everyone began to call him, had bounced around baseball considerably. From the time he had signed in baseball in 1953 until he arrived with the Dodgers that May, his contract had been transferred 17 times.

Five days after he replaced Tommy Davis he hit a tenth-inning home run to beat Houston. Three days later he was beaned so badly that it crushed his protective helmet. He was only back a couple of days when he and Al Ferrara collided heavily in left center field, and Lou was giving away at least thirty pounds. Then on June 12 Al Jackson of the Cubs hit him and fractured his right thumb.

But you couldn't get Lou out of the lineup. A lot of folks called him our Cinderella Man. He refused to quit. Would never give up. Gave us everything he had every day. I think that can partly be attributed to the fact he had been in baseball a long time with only a couple of brief shots with the Cubs, Angels and Braves.

Lou did a great deal for our 1965 club. I thought the club was really depressed with Davis's loss and maybe felt they couldn't put it all together without him. Then Johnson came in and played equally as well, in some areas perhaps better than Davis, primarily because he had such tremendous hustle and was such a cheerleader all the time.

Sandy Koufax put it well after we'd won a real tight race. "Johnson's the guy," he told the press. "If it had not been for the job he did we might not be here today."

A lot of people go into the winning of pennants. One of the principal ones for us in 1965 was Sandy. He shut the Reds out September 29, 5–0, to eliminate them and give us a two-game lead on the Giants.

That's where we were the next Saturday (October 2) when I called on Sandy to face Milwaukee with just two days' rest. It was the next to the last day of the season. If we win we clinch the pennant. Sandy never questioned my call. He went out there and beat the Braves and we locked up the championship.

It's difficult to differentiate among various pennants, but this has to be among my most satisfying. We were playing catch-up all year. A lot of people didn't think we could do it. We had limited bat power. We had no one up among the top five in any hitting department but we had superb pitching from Koufax, Don Drysdale, Claude Osteen (who we obtained during the winter from Washington), and John Podres, plus our top re-liefers—Ron Perranoski and Bob Miller.

There was a lot of juggling going on all year. One of my best moves was to reactivate Jim Gilliam from coach to player status. He took over third base for 80 games of the 111 he played in and hit .280 for us. When you had Gilliam batting second behind Maury Wills you had a master at working with the man to steal—Maury stole 94 to lead the league—or hit behind the runner.

A lot of folks wrote us off in mid-September when the Giants took a two-game series from us that left us in third, 4½ games back. But with guys like Johnson, Koufax, Drysdale, Gilliam and the rest prodding things along, we took off on a streak, winning fifteen of our last sixteen, including thirteen in succession.

Sandy tied the bow around the pennant when he beat the Braves on a four-hitter for the clincher on the final Saturday.

In the last four games of our thirteen-game streak, Sweet Lou Johnson was something. He made 10 hits in 18 at bats for a .556 average. And who scored the winning run for Koufax? Johnson.

Winning the pennant left us ecstatic but it also brought a problem to the fore. The series against the Twins was to open on Wednesday in Milwaukee, but it was also Yom Kippur, the Jewish high holy day, and Koufax, a devout Jew, had never played baseball on this Day of Atonement.

Nor would I ask him. This was strictly his business and it was understood by all of us in the Dodger family. Some fans tried to put pressure on Sandy by going all the way to the top. Mr. O'Malley took care of that in his usual graceful fashion.

"I wouldn't let Sandy pitch on his Day of Atonement," he told the media who asked, "even if he wanted to."

We lost the opening game to the Twins, 8–2, with Don Drysdale, but maybe I made a mistake. Perhaps I should have let Don work a few innings in the final National League game on Sunday. With five days' rest he just wasn't as sharp.

Sandy didn't have much better success in the second game, losing, 5–1. After that game I think Sandy made one of his most classic comments. He wasn't real sharp, and it was bitter cold that day. But the Twins and Jim Kaat simply did more things right. When asked about the game Sandy said:

"Kaat and Minnesota just did a better job. I was trying to get by with anything I had. If I could have gotten somebody out by throwing up my cap I'd have done that too."

Not many people realized that Sandy has that little touch of soft, sly humor. It came out quite a bit around the players, and this remark was typical.

Now we were heading back to Chavez Ravine and Dodger Stadium. We were two down but several clubs had been in that position before and come back. I held a little meeting before the game on Saturday.

It was nothing big. I've never made much of an emotional appeal to the Dodgers in all my years. I used to try some of Knute Rockne's tactics when I was coaching high school basketball years and years ago but I figured these guys were pros, adults, and wouldn't buy any of that malarkey.

I told them how the 1955 club had been down, had come back and won. We also talked about our approach to hitting. Some of the fellows were trying for the fences. We got into the Series by just trying to meet the ball, to get singles. I asked them to cut down on their swing and just meet the ball. It seemed to work.

Claude Osteen did the job, shutting out the Twins, 4–0, so we were one back. In game four we took it to them the way we'd done all year by bunting and running, and Drysdale won, 7–2, to square everything. Lou Johnson helped out with an eighth-inning home run.

I kind of liked the way things stood. It was like starting a new three-game series. I had Sandy to go in game five and Osteen in six. "If it goes beyond that," I told the writers, "I'll wait and see."

Sandy was pretty sharp. The first dozen that faced him found only air. We got four runs the first four innings. Minnesota ended up with four hits but were blanked, 7–0, as Sandy walked only one and struck out ten.

Koufax created a little incident in the sixth inning that set the 55,801 in Dodger Stadium roaring. We didn't know what it was all about until afterwards. Joe Garagiola, who was broadcasting the game, made some remark but we couldn't hear it.

"I could hear the transistors from the crowd," Koufax told Joe afterwards, "but I didn't catch what you said."

"All I said," Joe explained, "was something about 'There stands the greatest pitcher in baseball hitching up his pants before 55,000 fans. He must have a bad tailor.'"

It was a typical masterful effort by Koufax. The kind you expected as routine and when one didn't come you were a little startled. Sam Mele, who was managing Minnesota in 1965, added to Koufax's luster.

"No doubt about it," said Sam, "he's amazing, the best I ever saw, though I didn't see Bob Feller and some of the others at their peak."

When Mudcat Grant beat Osteen and a few others in game six, 5–1, at Minnesota, it all came down to sudden death. There were no more tomorrows. Throughout the first six innings of that sixth game Koufax was in the clubhouse getting treatments from Trainer Wayne Anderson. Sandy had volunteered to be ready to relieve if we had a chance to catch the Twins even though it would be with only a day's rest.

But things never turned that way. Now the monkey was on my back. Sandy would have two days' rest by Thursday (October 14). Drysdale, with a full three days, was fully rested, and by logic it was his turn.

"It will either be Sandy or Drysdale," I told the press afterwards. "I won't decide until morning. Maybe not until game time. I want to think about it."

I didn't tell them or anyone else either that I had whispered to Koufax during the ninth inning of the sixth game that if everything was right—conditions, his arm, etc.—that I'd probably start him. I asked him at the same time to say nothing to anyone. But I wanted Sandy to know.

After all the media had cleared the clubhouse I called Sandy and Don in one at a time and talked with them. Then I talked to them together. I explained my thinking. It was simple. The book dictated that I start Koufax, a left-hander, over Drysdale, a right-hander.

If we started Don, Sandy would have to be in the bullpen. Because of the arthritis in his arm it took Sandy longer to warm up. Suppose we went that route and had to bring Sandy in to relieve. Then we had to bat for him in case of a tight situation. My best bullpen man was a left-hander, Perranoski.

By going with Koufax, Mele had to go with his best right-handed hitting batting order. If Sandy got in trouble, we'd bring in Don. Then Mele would have to switch to some left-handed batters. That would set up my best reliever, Perranoski, who would force Mele to scramble with whatever he had left.

Koufax told me his arm felt fine. When the media asked him he gave them the same answer. But I liked his postscript best.

"If Walt asks me to pitch," he said, "I'm not going out there to lose."

Koufax was not the insurmountable Koufax he could be, but in a clutch game he was up to any assignment. We knew early

186

in the game that his curve ball wasn't breaking. He couldn't get it over, so he pitched the last four innings with his fast ball and that alone.

"It can't be done unless you are exceptional," John Roseboro, who caught Sandy, said afterwards. "And Sandy is the most exceptional pitcher in the game today."

When you remember that he blanked the Twins on three hits—only Frank Quilici's double being for extra bases—walked three and struck out ten, you realize it was an exceptional game by an exceptional man.

Another exceptional guy staked Sandy to the only run he needed, although we added another in the same inning on Wes Parker's single that scored Ron Fairly.

Sweet Lou was the exceptional man with a home-run shot off Kaat. Lou missed one of Kaat's changes, but then Kaat came back with a low fast ball and Johnson drove it out of the park. It was a remarkable year for a remarkable guy who gave us everything he had every day.

Now you would think there would be at least one disappointed man on this club that day—Drysdale. He was up a time or two but never made the mound. But I think he was one of the first out there to shake Sandy's hand when he fanned Bob Allison for his tenth strikeout and his 131st pitch of the game.

After all the champagne was gone and all the media and well-wishers had cleared the clubhouse so they could move around, Drysdale and Koufax met at their side-by-side lockers.

"You beautiful, beautiful fellow," Don yelled out as he and Sandy hugged. Two remarkable guys, two remarkable pitchers, and, looking back on 1965, a remarkable year for every one of the Dodgers. Me included.

The Associated Press named me Manager of the Year. They've given me that honor six times over the years, United Press International five times and *The Sporting News* three times. You wonder sometimes just what it all means. I do know it is appreciated, but when you look around at all the fine men managing in baseball you wonder how some of them would do if they had all the talent on our club.

I often think of a remark John Wooden, UCLA's phenomenal basketball coach, made to me once. "Coaches don't win championships, players do." That is true. Oh, a coach or a manager can help, but the best one alive can't do a thing if he hasn't got the talent.

That's why I kiddingly tell those who ask if I'm in Who's Who that I am but my players put me there. I don't even remember exactly when I was included, but it was somewhere along in the mid-60s when I had all those fellows like Koufax, Drysdale, Wills, Parker, Gilliam, Osteen, Roseboro, Lou Johnson—fellows like that who make a manager look good.

One thing about that championship in 1965—it eliminated one question real early. Usually I didn't even think about a contract for the next season—like 1966—until we were done or, more often than not, when I arrived at training camp in Vero Beach.

Back in the last few days in July I was sitting in my office talking with Sid Ziff of the *Los Angeles Times* and a few of the Cincinnati writers when the phone rang.

"Congratulations," Buzzie Bavasi said when I said hello. "You've been rehired for the 1966 season along with your whole staff."

That was the earliest I'd ever been given my new contract. I was stunned a little bit by it. Not by being rehired—I never have thought about not being the Dodger manager—but by the sudden way it happened. But I was pleased, and I know my coaches were. Later on one of the writers was needling Buzzie about giving me a raise and I got as big a kick out of that conversation as the new contract.

As I've said, I've never had a problem about money with the Dodgers and Mr. O'Malley and they took good care of me for 1966 and all the other years.

Little did any of us realize going home with our World Series triumph just what 1966 would mean to the Dodgers and each of us.

We came up with a start along about packing time for spring training when Koufax and Drysdale decided to hold out as a tandem. Since contract negotiations are between the players and the front office I've never taken sides. I'm sure not taking sides now.

All I know is that when we arrived in Vero Beach the last week in February there was a giant hole where our pitching staff was supposed to be. As the days went by and nothing seemed to happen that would bring the players and the club closer together, I could foresee a long season despite some youngsters who were coming.

One of those, Don Sutton, then barely twenty-one, had only a year of minor league experience. He'd won eight and lost one with Santa Barbara in the California League. Then as he moved up to Albuquerque, he was 15 and 6 with a 2.78 ERA. Don went on to win a starting berth after that brief experience. He might not have made it if Sandy and Don Drysdale had been in camp all the way. We gave Sutton a thorough trial, and by early June he was 7 and 4.

When we pulled stakes in Vero Beach on March 31 with neither Koufax or Drysdale in sight and seemingly little hope of signing, I resigned myself to playing the 1966 season without them, or at least for a good part of the way.

We flew out of Vero for Arizona to close out preseason preparation with some exhibitions with the clubs who trained there. Suddenly on April 2, Buzzie Bavasi called to tell me he had reached a compromise with Koufax and Drysdale for $100,000-plus contracts and they would be flying over.

The size of their contracts was no concern of mine but their arms were. It was a joyful reunion for all of us when they arrived that day. I was very dubious of just when they would be in shape. The next day it was evident that Drysdale had been working out, throwing a bit and running while a holdout.

Sandy told me right off that he had done some running, but the last time he had picked up a baseball to throw was the last game of the World Series on October 14. A controlled, conservative but crash program of training was ordered for both.

Three days later in an exhibition with the Giants, Don worked three innings. He allowed five hits and three earned runs but didn't look too bad. Koufax came on in the same game, working the same number of innings—3—allowing five hits and two earned runs. He too looked pretty good, but hardly the overpowering Koufax we all remembered from 1965 when he was 26–8 and had a 2.04 ERA, 27 complete games, 335 innings pitched, set a major league record with 382 strikeouts and eight shutouts.

Koufax was confident he was ready. He assured me he could work in the first series with Houston, which he did and which we lost. But he was not the loser of record. Drysdale was a little slower coming around. He made his first start against Chicago on April 15 but he too was not the pitcher of record.

Sandy recorded his first victory April 17, beating the Cubs 2–1, although I took him out after six innings since I didn't want to take a chance on hurting his arm on a rather cold day. Drysdale recorded his first win a few days later, going the distance against Milwaukee. We appeared on our way, hopefully, toward another pennant.

I've been asked a hundred times since if that didn't prove spring training was too long. That it might not be necessary. Or if it shouldn't be only ten days or two weeks. I don't agree with that. These were two exceptional men, who took exceptional care of themselves during the off-season and possessed seldom-equaled talents.

Spring training is vital for all, but particularly for a pitcher. It gets him in prime shape and allows him to bring his arm back gradually, generally in a warm climate and controlled conditions. It also enables him to work on his control, new pitches, his delivery and all the other things so vital to success.

I would be opposed to a shortened training period, especially for a pitcher. Obviously, Koufax and Drysdale proved it might be reduced a bit. But the reduction should come for established pitchers like a Koufax or a Drysdale.

With so few minor leagues in existence now, spring training is the only grounds for a club to instruct youngsters coming up, or to recondition veterans to the little things that make for champions. And it is the place to experiment if you want to switch a man's position as we did when we moved Bill Russell from the outfield to shortstop.

I never agreed with the joint holdout of Koufax and Drysdale and told them so. It accomplished their purpose but raised havoc with the team's overall preparation and planning. Nevertheless I still think baseball contracts are for individual negotiations and the sooner the better. I know of a lot of players who don't like spring training but the experience of thousands has proved it valuable.

Both Drysdale and Koufax told me later in the year that their late signing and later arrival put a tremendous burden on both of them. It was their opinion that owners should reach earlier settlements and not allow long holdouts to develop. The accelerated pace of preparation to pitch put too much of a burden on them overall and their arms in particular.

By early June Koufax was the Koufax of old. He was off to his greatest start in his career with a 10–1 record. Drysdale, on the other hand, seemed to have greater problems getting his fast ball back and his control under command. He had a 4–5 record for the same point in time.

1966 was another of those seasons like 1965 where no club really took command. Ultimately it settled down to a four-team race with no one dominating. The lead changed hands often among the Giants, Pirates, Reds and us. I don't recall how often we were in first, but we were in and out and up and down through most of the season.

I remember we were as far down as sixth once or twice in the early days of the season, with the lead flopping back and forth among the Pirates, Giants and Dodgers. Along about the second week of September we took a narrow lead away from the Pirates when Bob Miller beat Houston, and we hung on from there to the end.

Literally we hung on. We never led by more than 3½ games and never less than one, but we went right down to the final Sunday in Philadelphia before we won it. Then it was in the final game of a doubleheader. We had to send Koufax out to do it with only two days' rest.

It was a three-cornered fight until a day or two before when Pittsburgh was eliminated. I'd hoped we could have won it in the first game that Sunday in old Connie Mack Stadium in Phillie but Chris Short edged Bob Miller in a tight one, 4–3. Drysdale had started but lasted only a couple of innings and Miller finished up. Still, we couldn't get the runs we needed.

I had hoped to rest Sandy, but that last game was just like a World Series finale for us. If we lost there'd be a playoff and possibly no tomorrow, so Sandy got my call.

Koufax went out there in considerable pain from the arthritis in his elbow against Jim Bunning, a tough pitcher in any game but especially tough with all the chips on the line. We got to him in the early innings and built up a 6–0 lead when Bunning departed.

Sandy had been in several jams during the early innings but

got out of them all. Then in the ninth Richie Allen was safe on an error, and Harvey Kuenn singled to left. Tony Taylor singled to score Allen and Bill White followed with a double to bring in Kuenn and Taylor.

Three runs were in; no one was out. Sandy was tired but still he was the best we had and you stick with your best. In those next few pitches Sandy showed more courage than probably any other time. He reached back for everything he had. He fanned Bob Uecker and then got Bobby Wine to ground out to short. With Jackie Brandt the batter, Sandy fired a fast ball past him that Brandt never saw for his tenth strikeout of the day, a 6–3 victory and back-to-back pennants for the third time in Dodger history.

None of us knew it then but it was Sandy's last victory in a Dodger uniform. The game didn't end until 7:10 P.M. Philadelphia time. While there was a lot of champagne being poured, none of the guys objected a bit to waiting for Sandy to go through that horrible ordeal of icing down his arm.

We didn't reach International Airport until 4 A.M. and much to our surprise there were several hundred fans patiently waiting for us to arrive. It was a good feeling even though we had won the pennant three times in the last four years. When that many people stay up that late to meet a baseball team you just know they're true fans.

Once more they mobbed Koufax, who was superb despite that brief letdown in the ninth inning. His fast ball was so quick that last game. Drysdale told the press that "Sandy's fast ball was unbelievable," but that often was the case with Sandy.

As hard as it is to believe, Sandy was better in '66 than '65. He won 27 and lost 9 for a 75 percent winning factor, had a 1.73 ERA, started 41 games and completed 27. In 323 innings he struck out 317 and he pitched five shutouts. The only thing he didn't do was match the perfect game he threw against the Cubs in '65.

We were favored against the Orioles and they beat us to death. It was almost like a tennis match: 2–5, 0–6, 0–1 and 0–1.

The Robinsons, Frank and Brooks, bombed us out in the first game with back-to-back home runs off Don Drysdale that landed only a few feet apart in the left field pavilion in Dodger Stadium.

Then we managed to counter the six Baltimore runs in the second game with six errors—three in the fifth inning—and Koufax's string of 22 scoreless Series innings ended. A lot of people jumped all over Willie Davis for his three errors in that inning but we all came to his defense.

Sandy became particularly irritated with some TV interviewer when we were going to Baltimore. We all knew we wouldn't have been in the series without Willie Davis.

Willie lost both balls in the sun and shirts of the crowd in that fifth inning. Ironically, I had told the media in our workout the day before the series started that I felt the series should be played at night. "Most games during the season are at night," I commented, "so why change for the Series? Playing conditions are better. You don't have those white shirts to contend with nor the glare of the sun."

The Series planners have gone to night games during the week, for which I am thankful. I only wish it had happened several years before.

Headed for Baltimore and down two, we were faced with the reality that only five clubs in history had ever come back to win, two of them Dodgers in 1955 and 1965. But it wasn't to be.

We were out of it in four, and now we all knew how the Yankees felt when we ripped them in 1963 in four straight. It is a devastating way to lose, but when you score only two runs in four games and are shut out the last thirty-three innings, all you can do is go away and come to play another day.

In our case that other day would have to wait until the next year. And once again we were committed to a tour of Japan, a five-week jaunt that none of us looked forward to, especially after being skunked.

One of the writers asked me what I was going to say at all those press conferences in Japan about losing the Series in four straight.

"I'm going to tell them I can't understand what they're saying."

29

BACK-TO-BACK championships in 1965 and 1966 were things you liked to look back on. But none of us were really ready for the postscript to the 1966 season, even though all of us were aware of the problems Sandy Koufax had pitched under for several years.

We had discussed it many times, but when the word came on November 18, 1966, it was Black Friday for the Dodgers, for all of baseball, but particularly for the fans.

Sandy Koufax's retirement ended one of the greatest careers in the game. Some writers called him the greatest pitcher ever. I'll tell you he was the greatest I've seen but "ever" takes in a long time and one person hasn't seen them all.

I can say this. If somehow every pitcher in baseball history could be taken back to his prime and were ready to pitch, my first choice from among them would be Koufax.

A lot of people faulted Sandy for quitting. I never did. Sure, he would have helped us in 1967 and maybe for several years after that. But I had known for a long time that he pitched in great pain. Only he could make the decision, and I told him that several times.

He retired at his peak and he had given us a great effort for twelve years. If throwing another baseball had left his arm crippled that would have been a terrible price to pay for continuing. You could never ask more of any player than Sandy gave. A very intelligent pitcher and an equally bright man, Sandy put it well when he announced his retirement: "I don't regret for one minute the twelve years I've spent in baseball but I could regret one season too many."

194

It was a dark hour for the Dodgers and for me personally. Not only was Sandy a phenomenal pitcher but, as with most of our players, I really liked the guy.

Many people in the years that followed felt our sudden drop from first to eighth in 1967 was because of the loss of Koufax. No doubt it contributed. You don't lose a 27-game winner with a 1.73 ERA and not feel it. But we also traded Tommy Davis and Maury Wills, and along with the little things in baseball, we tailed off.

We had our problems for two years, finishing seventh in 1968. But then the youngsters in our farm system began to come together and while we never won the pennant until 1974, we finished fourth, second, second, third, second and first in '74.

That seven-year span was the longest we'd been without a pennant in my years. It proves one thing. Walter O'Malley is a patient man. We were a contender all those years after dropping way back but a number of things just didn't allow us to put it together.

Now, we could write two or three books on all the ifs, ands, and buts in baseball, but that wouldn't change the standings in any of those years or any of the scores.

Somewhere back in those years I read a survey done on National League managers' average length of service since 1940 and it came out to 2.8 years on the job. Now I've beat that by a considerable margin, and as long as Mr. O'Malley and Peter want me, my health is good, and I continue to enjoy the job, I'm going to stick around.

Where else could you find a finer life? I sure don't know.

Every once in a while—really more often than that—I'm asked about working with a one-year contract. I've never worried about it from the first day I signed on. Anything longer might make me nervous. A lot of managers sign those "long-term" agreements and the next thing you know they're gone.

I'll just continue to play it this way.

In those seven years without a pennant we seemed to have all the ingredients—even in 1967 and 1968—but frustrations pursued us every season. We were right up there in 1970. Then in 1971 we went down to the wire again with the Giants before losing out by a game.

But everything came together in 1974. After the first few days of the season when we shuffled back and forth between first and second with the Giants, we led all the way. At one point just before the All-Star break we led by 10½ games, though we let that slip, winning out over the Reds by four games.

We helped ourselves during the winter after the 1974 season. In December while the winter baseball meetings were on, Al Campanis made a trade with Montreal that cost us Willie Davis but brought us Mike Marshall, a relief pitcher who thrived on work.

A day or two later Al filled the hole that was left in center-field when he traded Claude Osteen to Houston for Jimmy Wynn, an established centerfielder who could hit a pretty good long ball.

Two trades the year before had been beneficial as well. We swapped Richie Allen for Tommy John, a strong left-handed pitcher, and Frank Robinson, Bill Singer, Billy Grabarkewitz, Mike Strahler and Bobby Valentine for Andy Messersmith and a former Dodger, Ken McMullen.

There was a lot of talk that I didn't get along with Richie Allen and Frank Robinson. Not true. Allen never caused me any real trouble. We had a little bit in common—we both loved horses—and we talked about them a good bit. People claimed that I objected because Allen didn't take batting practice. I've never believed too much in batting practice anyway and as long as he hit where it counted—in the game—that was OK with me. Some of our guys objected, but no two men are alike, and when the game started Richie gave you 100 percent.

Robinson was no big problem either. He was kind of a moody guy, but a lot of people are. You learn to live with them. Frank was a sound baseball man. He still swung a good bat though by the time he came to us he had lost a lot of his speed.

In our park, however, pitching is vital and when we could add a left-hander like John and a right-hander like Messersmith I was all for the trades.

With the talent our farm system developed and the considerable amount from outside that John, Messersmith, Marshall and Wynn added, the 1974 Dodgers were a solid team.

Our line-up was an intriguing one. We split up our catching between Steve Yeager and Joe Ferguson. When Fergie wasn't catching he was in right field against left-handed pitchers.

A number of our regulars were converts. Steve Garvey, who had a rough time trying to make it at third base, moved to first and became so proficient he was voted the most valuable player in the National League.

Davey Lopes, whose speed kept opposing pitchers in a dither, was converting from an outfielder to second base. Bill Russell came from the outfield to shortstop, where he did a tremendous job both in the field and at bat.

Once Garvey was cleared from third, Ron Cey became solid there, giving us a fine defensive man and a good bat. My old buddie Red Patterson reached back in those statistics of his to tell the world that Ronnie was the forty-fifth man to play third since the club came to Los Angeles. Red was always coming up with some number like that for the media.

Our left fielder in '74 was Bill Buckner. He had come up in our system as a first baseman, but Garvey had come along so well at first and Buck could play the outfield so well that it was a natural move.

Wynn handled center, but way back in his career he had broken in as a shortstop so he too was converted. As I said Fergie was in right against left-handers and Willie Crawford against right-handers.

Our pitching staff was strong and experienced: Don Sutton, Tommy John, and Andy Messersmith with Al Downing, Doug Rau and Geoff Zahn working the fourth spot. Then we had Mike Marshall, Jim Brewer and Charlie Hough in relief. We had fine depth and a lot of ways to go.

We could even count Marshall among the converts since he was a shortstop in his early years before becoming a pitcher. Mike had long thrived on work but in 1974 he set a major league mark, appearing in 208 innings in 106 games with a 15–12 record and a 2.42 ERA.

That was a phenomenal effort for a relief pitcher. Because of it he won the Cy Young award in 1974 and was the first relief pitcher in 24 years to win the *Sporting News* Pitcher of the Year honor.

Going into the 1974 season we were a team to contend with. We had none of the so-called superstars although some of our guys like Garvey and Marshall sure came on. We did things a little differently in the spring and to read about it you'd have thought it was a revolution. I decided to have a formal session with each man at Vero Beach early on, a private session where we could go over our objectives, our training program, what we felt were our strengths and our weaknesses and similar things as they pertained to each man.

I was concerned because we were young and didn't have a lot of experience. In fact, there was more than a lot of inexperience at the jobs we were asking guys to handle. So I knew if we were to win it would have to be a total effort as a team by the twenty-five who made the roster.

The toughest thing about baseball is sitting on the bench. You wait and you wait and you wait, hoping that the skipper will give you the chance you want. Then you go out there and in one day you feel you've got to sell him.

I know how it is. I went through it a long, long time ago but it was no different then than now. So I hoped to provide each of our guys with a little more insight into what we wanted to accomplish.

And I guess you could say we did accomplish our objectives. We won 102 games and beat out a real strong Cincinnati club managed by my old friend Sparky Anderson by four games. The Reds won 98 games but second place put them out of the playoffs. Yet Pittsburgh, who won the Eastern Division by a game and a half, was able to win only 88. The Reds won 60.5 percent of their games, the Pirates 54.3 percent, yet Cincinnati was only a spectator.

I have divided feelings about the playoff system. First off, when you have this many clubs in the league, I think it is a good idea. It holds the players' interest as well as the fans and it's good for baseball in general. The only bad thing about it is that you might have the best club in baseball—based on your season's record—and not be in the Series.

Or, as in Cincinnati's case in 1974, you're the second best club in the National League based on performance but you're shut out because the best club has a great year and they're in your division. I still feel if you win more games than anyone else in baseball you should be in the World Series. But if you have a bad playoff series you won't make it.

The system, while it increases player interest, also puts an additional burden on them. It used to be a big thing when you won the pennant. You were in the World Series. Now you're just in the championship playoff and you'd better keep that momentum going or you'll be watching the big one on the tube.

We made it to the Series by taking a good Pittsburgh team three games to one. It was a big series that attracted a lot of attention, and we got fine pitching from Sutton, Messersmith and Marshall.

A bomb scare attracted a lot of attention too, most of all, ours.

When we got to the airport from the ball park to fly home we were delayed on the ground for several hours while they checked out a threat that a bomb had been planted aboard the Dodger plane. Of course, it was a false alarm but it had to be done.

It had been a big year and now we had what counted ahead of us. We had played excellent ball through most of 1974 but like every year little things happen to create an incident and they're blown all out of proportion.

I remember a Sunday night in Philadelphia after we had lost a tight 3–2 game to the Phils in the ninth inning. Some of the players were in the lounge of the Marriott Hotel and got a little loud playing liar's poker, a game in which the serial numbers on dollar bills are used to form poker hands. Some little old ladies complained to the manager and the security man was called. The next call was to me.

Now I wasn't in any mood for a problem after we had lost the game. I couldn't take the players' part. Actually I didn't even want to hear their side. I just told them that if I had played like they had I'd be up in my room with the pillows over my head. I told them to go to their rooms, and, since it was about 8:30, it probably was the earliest curfew in baseball.

The next day, in talking with the hotel staff and the players, I found that perhaps I'd been a little hasty. Apparently the players weren't totally at fault. They weren't that loud, but at the time I was in no mood for anything, especially a hassle with some little old ladies.

Now I overreacted and so did the hotel people, and the writers traveling with us had a ball turning the story into a headline at home. Indirectly, the hassle seemed to have an impact in bringing everyone together. We led by 1½ games after that loss and after two days of rain in Montreal began a run that took us to a 7½ game lead in ten days.

I was extremely happy for the players. They'd taken quite a bit of abuse from a lot of quarters the year before when we lost out to the Reds in the final weeks of September. We had led from the middle of June in 1973 until the 4th of September when Cincinnati took over.

I was quite irritated with our critics then. The Reds were a tremendous ball club. They won 99 games and people were saying my guys choked. Now you don't choke when you win 95 games like we did to finish second. That was thirteen more than the Mets won in taking the Eastern Division, so when we came back in 1974 to beat out almost the identical Reds club and they won 98 games, you know we had ourselves quite a season.

Oakland won out in the American League for the third season in a row, and they were a problem. In spite of all kinds of talk about their clubhouse fights and rebellion against their owner, Charlie Finley, they played baseball like champions.

We, on the other hand, didn't play as well in the Series as we did in the playoffs or during the regular season, but that's one of the real dangers of a short Series. You can quit hitting, as we did against Baltimore in 1966, or your pitching can go flat.

We met the ball well enough to win the first game, getting 11 hits, but only Jimmy Wynn's home run got any big ones on the board as we lost, 3–2. We left twelve runners on base, three in the fifth inning, when we got an unearned run on two Oakland errors.

As our players said afterwards, "They didn't win it, we lost it." We hit the ball well. But each time it was right at them or it was a double play.

That game produced one of the most remarkable pegs from the outfield that I have ever seen. It came in the eighth inning. Jimmy Wynn was in center with an arm that was due to have surgery after the Series. Sal Bando was on third, Reggie Jackson at bat.

Jackson lofted a towering fly to medium right center. It was Wynn's ball to play. Jimmy and Joe Ferguson had an agreement, however, that if Joe could get to a ball he'd take it since all Jimmy could do was kind of sail the ball back into the infield.

200

As Bando tagged up to go on his coach's call, Fergie cut in front of Wynn at the last split second. Bando cut loose for the plate and Fergie threw the ball on the line dead to Steve Yeager guarding the plate to beat the sliding Bando.

That peg sent Dodger Stadium into an uproar, and rightly so. It was a perfect throw. It showed the advantage of flexibility. If Willie Crawford had been in right he might have got the ball, but, being left-handed, in this case he would have had to stop and pivot to make the throw. Joe just cocked his arm and fired the strike.

It was the bright spot of the day, but it didn't make up for the defeat. Nothing does, no matter what you do. The old saying that defeat is bitter is true. Always.

Oakland got only six hits off Messersmith and Marshall, but that's baseball. They got the most runs. You've got to get your hits at the right time. It all evens up. We win some that way too but in a short stand like a World Series it's different.

We evened things up on Sunday, giving Don Sutton a tight 3–2 win. The defensive star of Saturday was the offensive hero of Sunday. Fergie tied into one of Vida Blue's fast balls in the sixth. It was one of the hardest hit balls in my memory at Dodger Stadium. It went out over the 420 sign in centerfield, and from the sunken dugout it looked like it was just about as high.

Oakland rallied in the ninth to score two runs and bring Mike Marshall to work. It was here that a little pupil and professor byplay went on. Mike teaches in the Physical Education department at Michigan State. Two of his former students were our Steve Garvey and Herb Washington, a world-class track man and Oakland's designated runner.

Washington came in to run for Joe Rudi at first. Marshall, who has one of the great moves to first base for a right-handed pitcher, stepped off the mound a time or two just to keep Washington alert. When this speedster comes in it's for only one purpose—steal.

He'd been in 92 games during the season but had never been to bat; yet he stole 28 bases, so he had a gift for the task. Mike kept Washington jumping back and forth as he stepped off the rubber a few times. Then he made a peg to Garvey, who almost got his former Michigan State classmate.

201

Then Marshall gave him his great motion. Washington started to go, saw the pickoff peg, and wheeled in his tracks, but Garvey had him beat by a foot or two. It was quite a show and the spectators loved it. So did we, because Mike struck out Angel Mangual and the Series was even.

After a day's rest we moved into the Oakland Coliseum for game three. I had to do a little wrestling with myself. Doug Rau had been pitching third in our rotation late in the season but had had trouble. I decided to go with Al Downing. We had used him as a spot starter, and he had won five for us in the National League, his last being an impressive 11–0 shutout against the Giants.

We didn't give Al a lot of support as we lost that game, 3–2. Errors gave the A's two unearned runs, and in these short affairs you can't give too much away or you're going to end up short, as we did.

It was a similar game to the opener. We hit the ball hard but right at them. Three or four line shots were just outs instead of sharp singles or extra base hits. Ironically, after three games every one had ended 3–2, only the winners changed and now Oakland was up by a game.

The hits were even in game four at seven but the runs went to Oakland, 5–2. Now we were in trouble, being down by three with three to go and needing them all to win. Their pitcher, Ken Holtzman, helped himself with a home run over the left field fence in the third.

But we helped him even more with some misplays in the sixth that gave them four runs. Holtzman's home run was only the third in his career, and it was even more distinctive since during the American League season he didn't even bat because of the designated hitter rule.

We were down to a one-game situation. We had to win every one or be out. We had a little meeting before the fifth game. I don't try to give pep talks. I don't think that works in baseball, which is a touch game. I just reminded all the players that we were a much better team over the long haul than we had shown in this short series.

I told them we were good enough to win three straight and take it but it would take a great effort by every one of us. We

202

gave our best, but again it wasn't good enough or perhaps Oakland was just better.

There were a lot of critics of Bill Buckner for his base running in the eighth inning when we were trailing 3–2 and no one was out. After he singled, Buck, who has great instincts on the bases, continued to second on an error, then tried to stretch it to three bases as Bill North continued to bobble the ball.

He was cut down by a perfect combination—a shot thrown from Reggie Jackson to Dick Green to Sal Bando. Now the critics insisted we'd have been better off if Buck had held up at second since there were no outs.

It turned out to be a mistake, of course. But if Buck had made it, and he'd done it several times, it would have been a great move. I wish he hadn't gone, but I tell you this, I want aggressive players and Buckner is that. I would rather have them aggressive and try to corral them a bit than have to try and make them aggressive.

I didn't blame Buckner then, and I don't blame him now. We might have scored a run to tie it up and we might not have.

We were eliminated, again by a 3–2 score, but 1974 was a championship season by a young team that did far more things right than they did wrong. We'd much rather have had the full winners' shares at $22,219, but you're still the second best team in baseball and $15,703 is a nice round figure to take home.

You always want to be the best no matter what you do in life. But there's only one champion each year in baseball. I've been in baseball over forty years, twenty-three as manager of the Dodgers; we've won seven pennants and four times been the World Champions.

We've done it with experienced veterans, a mixture of a little of both and this last time mainly with youngsters.

Baseball has been mighty good to me and to all the fellows who've ever played the game. One of the great jobs when you're sixty plus is to watch those green young kids come up and grow into strong, vital young men who are all the while improving as players and making the most of their potential.

That's why I so enjoy this game and all that goes with playing it, like I always have—one year at a time.

Acknowledgements

My thanks to my wife, Lela; my daughter, Dodie; my son-in-law, Harry Ogle; my granddaughter, Kim; and my grandson, Rob; all of whom helped me reconstruct various facets in my life.

My grateful appreciation to Jack Tobin, who spent so many hours of interview with me in the preparation of this book.

Our thanks also go to Louisa Miller, who transcribed all of the tapes; to Mrs. Pat Wienandt, who edited the final script; and to Floyd Thatcher, vice president and executive editor of Word Books, who guided the entire project to its conclusion.

Appendix A

CAREER RECORD OF WALTER EMMONS ALSTON

Born December 1, 1911, at Butler County, O.

Height, 6.02. Weight, 210.

Threw and batted righthanded.

Hobbies—Hunting and woodworking

Attended Miami University, Oxford, O.; received Bachelor of Science degree in Physical Education.

Named Major League Manager of the Year by THE SPORTING NEWS, 1955, 1959 and 1963.

RECORD AS PLAYER

Year	Club	League	Pos.	G	AB	R	H	2B	3B	HR	RBI	BA	PO	A	E	FA
1935—Greenwood	E. Dixie	3B	82	319	46	104	25	11	1	46	.326	94	172	27	.908
1936—Huntington	M.At.	1-O-2B	120	482	89	157	16	8	*35	114	.326	900	91	22	.978
1936—St. Louis	Nat.	1B	1	1	0	0	0	0	0	0	.000	1	0	1	.500
1937—Rochester	Int.	1B	66	203	20	50	6	3	6	36	.246	472	43	6	.988
1937—Houston	Tex.	1B	65	208	20	44	9	1	0	16	.212	592	46	1	.998
1938—Portsmouth	Mid. Atl.	1B	122	444	76	138	22	3	28	106	.311	1084	56	9	•.992
1939—Portsmouth	Mid. Atl.	1B	2	6	1	2	0	0	0	0	.333	21	0	1	.955
1939—Columbus	Sally	1B	105	399	69	129	26	8	11	82	.323	982	51	6	*.994
1940—Portsmouth	Mid. Atl.	1B	127	446	79	122	18	3	*28	112	.274	1015	77	14	.987
1941—Springfield	Mid. Atl.	1B	125	456	*88	131	26	4	*25	*102	.287	1135	*86	13	*.989
1942—Springfield	Mid. Atl.	1B	129	462	54	143	16	3	*12	*90	.310	*1117	*106	12	•.990
1943—Rochester	Int.	1B-3B	115	313	37	75	12	2	5	40	.240	551	75	13	.980
1944—Rochester	Int.	1B-2B	13	19	2	3	0	0	0	2	.158	29	2	1	.969
1944—Trenton	Int.-St.	1B	52	180	46	63	10	2	9	48	.350	428	37	8	.983
1945—Trenton	Int.-St.	1B	126	447	91	140	30	4	14	93	.313	947	*74	12	*.988
1946—Nashua	N. Eng.	1B	50	165	21	43	5	6	2	30	.261	327	26	3	.992
1947—Pueblo	West.	PH	2	1	0	0	0	0	0	0	.000	0	0	0	.000
Major League Totals			1	1	0	0	0	0	0	0	.000	1	0	1	.500

RECORD AS MANAGER

Year	Club	League	Position	W	L	Year	Club	League	Position	W	L
1940—Portsmouth	Mid. Atl.	Sixth		59	68	1958—Los Angeles	Nat.	Seventh		71	83
1941—Springfield	Mid. Atl.	Fourth		69	57	1959—Los Angeles	Nat.	ᶜFirst		88	68
1942—Springfield	Mid. Atl.	Fifth		59	71	1960—Los Angeles	Nat.	Fourth		82	72
1944—Trenton†	Int.-St.	Sixth		31	18	1961—Los Angeles	Nat.	Second		89	65
1945—Trenton	Int.-St.	Third		70	69	1962—Los Angeles	Nat.	ᵈSecond		102	63
1946—Nashua	N. Eng.	‡Second		80	41	1963—Los Angeles	Nat.	First		99	63
1947—Pueblo	West.	§Third		70	58	1964—Los Angeles	Nat.	ᵉSixth		80	82
1948—St. Paul	A. A.	xThird		86	68	1965—Los Angeles	Nat.	First		97	65
1949—St. Paul	A. A.	yFirst		93	60	1966—Los Angeles	Nat.	First		95	67
1950—Montreal	Int.	Second		86	67	1967—Los Angeles	Nat.	Eighth		73	89
1951—Montreal	Int.	zFirst		95	59	1968—Los Angeles	Nat.	ᵉSeventh		76	86
1952—Montreal	Int.	ªFirst		95	56	1969—Los Angeles	Nat.	Fourth(W)		85	77
1953—Montreal	Int.	ᵇSecond		89	63	1970—Los Angeles	Nat.	Second(W)		87	74
1954—Brooklyn	Nat.	Second		92	62	1971—Los Angeles	Nat.	Second(W)		89	73
1955—Brooklyn	Nat.	First		98	55	1972—Los Angeles	Nat.	Third(W)		85	70
1956—Brooklyn	Nat.	First		93	61	1973—Los Angeles	Nat.	Second(W)		95	66
1957—Brooklyn	Nat.	Third		84	70	1974—Los Angeles	Nat.	First(W)		102	60
						1975—Los Angeles	Nat.	Second(W)		88	74

†Replaced Joe Bird with club in sixth place, July 28.
‡Won playoffs by defeating Pawtucket, three games to none and Lynn, four games to two.
§Won playoffs by defeating Des Moines, three games to one and Sioux City, four games to one.
xWon playoffs by defeating Indianapolis, four games to two and Columbus, four games to three; lost Junior World Series against Montreal (International League), four games to one.
yLost playoff semifinal series to Milwaukee, four games to three.
zWon playoffs by defeating Buffalo, four games to none and Syracuse, four games to one; lost Junior World Series against Milwaukee (American Association), four games to two.
ªLost playoff finals to Rochester, four games to two after defeating Toronto in semifinals, four games to three.
ᵇWon playoffs by defeating Buffalo, four games to two and Rochester, four games to none; won Junior World Series against Kansas City (American Association), four games to one.
ᶜDefeated Milwaukee Braves, two games to none in playoff for championship.
ᵈLost to San Francisco Giants, two games to one in playoff for championship.
ᵉTied for position.

CHAMPIONSHIP SERIES RECORD

Year	Club	League	W	L
1974	Los Angeles	National	3	1

WORLD SERIES RECORD

Year	Club	League	W	L
1955	Brooklyn	National	4	3
1956	Brooklyn	National	3	4
1959	Los Angeles	National	4	2
1963	Los Angeles	National	4	0
1965	Los Angeles	National	4	3
1966	Los Angeles	National	0	4
1974	Los Angeles	National	1	4

(Information in Appendix A is reprinted by courtesy of THE SPORTING NEWS.)

ROSTER OF DODGER PLAYERS DURING WALTER ALSTON'S TENURE AS MANAGER, 1954–

Name	Position	Year
Aguirre, Hank	P	1968
Alcaraz, Luis	IF	1967–68
Alexander, Doyle	P	1971
Allen, Richie	IF	1971
Alvarez, Orlando	OF	1973
Amoros, Sandy	OF	1952, 54–57, 59–60
Aspromonte, Bob	IF	1960–61
Auerbach, Rick	IF	1974–
Bailey, Bob	IF-OF	1967–68
Barbieri, Jim	OF	1966
Baxes, Jim	IF	1959
Belardi, Wayne	IF-OF	1954
Bessent, Don	P	1955–58
Bilko, Steve	IF	1958
Billingham, Jack	P	1968
Birrer, Bob	P	1958
Black, Joe	P	1954
Borkowski, Bob	OF	1955
Boyer, Ken	IF	1968–69
Breeding, Marv	IF	1963
Brewer, Jim	P	1964–75
Brubaker, Bruce	P	1967
Brumley, Mike	C	1957, 62–63
Buckner, Bill	IF-OF	1969–
Bunning, Jim	P	1969
Burright, Larry	IF	1962

Name	Position	Year
Calmus, Dick	P	1963
Camilli, Doug	C	1960–64
Campanella, Roy	C	1948–57
Campanis, Jim	C	1966–68
Cannizzaro, Chris	C	1972–73
Carey, Andy	IF	1962
Cey, Ron	IF	1971–
Churn, Clarence	P	1959
Cimoli, Gino	OF	1956–58
Colavito, Rocky	OF	1968
Collum, Jackie	P	1957–58
Covington, Wes	OF	1966
Cox, Billy	IF	1954
Craig, Roger	P	1955–61
Crawford, Willie	OF	1964–75
Culver, George	P	1973
Darnell, Bob	P	1954–56
Darwin, Bob	OF	1969–71
Davis, Tommy	IF-OF	1960–66
Davis, Willie	OF	1960–73
Dean, Tommy	IF	1967
De Jesus, Ivan	IF	1974–
Demeter, Don	OF	1956–61
Dietz, Dick	C	1972
Downing, Al	P	1971–
Drake, Solly	OF	1959

Name	Position	Year
Drysdale, Don	P	1958–69
Duffie, John	P	1967
Egan, Dick	P	1967
Ellingsen, Bruce	P	1972
Elston, Don	P	1957
Erskine, Carl	P	1948–59
Essegian, Chuck	OF	1959–60
Fairey, Jim	OF	1968, 73
Fairly, Ron	IF-OF	1958–69
Farrell, Dick	P	1961
Ferguson, Joe	C	1970–
Fernandez, Chico	IF	1956
Ferrara, Al	OF	1963, 65–68
Foster, Alan	P	1967–70
Fowler, Art	P	1959
Furillo, Carl	OF	1946–60
Gabrielson, Len	OF	1967–70
Garvey, Steve	IF-OF	1969–
Gentile, Jim	IF	1957–58
Giallombardo, Bob	P	1958
Gilliam, Jim	IF-OF	1953–66
Gleason, Roy	OF	1963
Golden, Jim	P	1960–61
Grabarkewitz, Bill	IF	1969–72
Grant, Jim	P	1968
Gray, Dick	IF	1958–59
Griffith, Derrell	IF-OF	1963–66
Hale, John	OF	1974–
Haller, Tom	C	1968–71
Hamrick, Odbert	OF	1955
Harkness, Tim	IF	1961–62
Harris, Bill	P	1957, 59
Heydeman, Greg	P	1973
Hickman, Jim	OF	1967
Hoak, Don	IF	1954–55
Hodges, Gil	IF-C-OF	1943–61
Hooton, Burt	P	1975–
Hopkins, Gail	C	1974
Hough, Charlie	P	1970–
Howard, Frank	IF-OF	1958–64
Howell, Dixie	C	1953, 55
Hudson, Rex	P	1974–
Hughes, Jim	P	1952–56
Hunt, Ron	IF	1967
Hunter, Willard	P	1962
Hutton, Tom	IF	1966, 69
Jackson, Ransom	IF	1956–58
James, Cleo	OF	1968
Jenkins, Jack	P	1969
John, Tommy	P	1972–
Johnson, Lou	OF	1965–67
Joshua, Von	OF	1969–71, 73–74
Kekich, Mike	P	1965, 68
Kellert, Frank	IF	1955
Kennedy, John	IF	1965–66
Kipp, Fred	P	1957–59
Klippstein, John	P	1958–59
Kosco, Andy	OF	1969–70
Koufax, Sandy	P	1955–66
Labine, Clem	P	1950–60
Lacy, Lee	IF-OF	1972–75
Lamb, Ray	P	1969–70

Name	Position	Year
Larker, Norm	IF-OF	1958–61
Lasorda, Tom	P	1954
Lee, Bob	P	1967
Lee, Leron	OF	1975–
Lefebvre, Jim	IF	1965–72
Lehman, Ken	P	1956
LeJohn, Don	IF	1965
Lewallyn, Dennis	P	1975–
Lillis, Bob	IF	1958–61
Loes, Billy	P	1950–55
Lopes, Davey	IF-OF	1972–
Maglie, Sal	P	1956–57
Manuel, Charlie	OF	1974–75
Marichal, Juan	P	1975
Marshall, Mike	P	1974–
Mauriello, Ralph	P	1958
McBean, Alvin	P	1969–70
McDermott, Terry	IF	1972
McDevitt, Danny	P	1958–60
McMullen, Ken	IF	1962–64, 73–75
Messersmith, Andy	P	1973–75
Meyer, Russ	P	1953–54
Michael, Gene	IF	1967
Miles, Don	OF	1958
Mikkelsen, Pete	P	1969–72
Miller, Bob	P	1963–67
Miller, John	IF	1969
Miller, Larry	P	1964
Miller, Rod	IF	1957
Milliken, Bob	P	1953–54
Mitchell, Dale	OF	1956
Moeller, Joe	P	1962–64, 66–71
Moon, Wally	OF	1959–65
Moore, Gary	IF	1970
Moryn, Walt	OF	1954–55
Mota, Manny	OF	1969–
Neal, Charlie	IF	1956–61
Negray, Ron	P	1958
Nelson, Rocky	IF	1952, 56
Nen, Dick	IF	1963
Newcombe, Don	P	1949–58
Noren, Irv	OF	1960
Norman, Fred	P	1970
O'Brien, Bob	P	1971
Oliver, Nate	IF	1963–67
Ortega, Phil	P	1960–64
Osteen, Claude	P	1965–73
Paciorek, Tom	IF-OF	1970–75
Palmquist, Ed	P	1960–61
Parker, Wes	IF-OF	1964–72
Pascual, Camilo	P	1970
Pasley, Kevin	C	1973–
Pena, Jose	P	1970–72
Perranoski, Ron	P	1961–67, 72
Pignatano, Joe	C	1958–60
Podres, Johnny	P	1958–66
Popovich, Paul	IF	1968–69
Powell, Paul Ray	C	1973, 75
Purdin, John	P	1964–65, 68–69
Rakow, Ed	P	1960
Rau, Doug	P	1972–
Reed, Howie	P	1964–66

211

Name	Position	Year
Werhas, John	IF	1964–65, 67
Wilhelm, Hoyt	P	1971–72
Willhite, Nick	P	1963–66
Williams, Dick	IF	1951–54
Williams, Stan	P	1958–62
Wills, Maury	IF	1959–66, 69–72
Wilson, Robert	OF	1958
Windhorn, Gordon	OF	1961
Wojey, Pete	P	1954
Wynn, Jimmy	OF	1974–75
Yeager, Steve	C	1972–
Zahn, Geoff	P	1973–75
Zimmer, Don	IF	1954–59, 63

The following have served as coaches for the Dodgers during Alston's tenure as manager beginning in 1954:

Adams, Red	1969–
Basgall, Monte	1973–
Becker, Joe	1955–64
Beringer, Carroll	1967–72
Bragan, Bobby	1960
Bryant, Clay	1961
Dressen, Charlie	1958–59
Durocher, Leo	1961–64
Gilliam, Jim	1965–
Gomez, Preston	1965–67
Hartsfield, Roy	1969–72
Herman, Billy	1954–57
Lasorda, Tom	1973–
Lyons, Ted	1954
Mulleavy, Greg	1957–60, 62–64
Ozark, Danny	1965–72
Phillips, Lefty	1965–68
Pitler, Jake	1954–57
Reese, Pee Wee	1959
Reiser, Pete	1960–64
Walker, Dixie	1970–74
Walker, Rube	1958